Children and stress

understanding and helping

Beverly Hardcastle Stanford
and
Kaoru Yamamoto,
Editors

Association for Childhood Education International
17904 Georgia Avenue, Suite 215
Olney, Maryland 20832
800-423-3563 • www.acei.org

Bruce Herzig, ACEI Editor
Anne W. Bauer, ACEI Editor
Deborah Jordan Kravitz, Production

17904 Georgia Ave., Ste. 215, Olney, MD 20832

Library of Congress Cataloging-in-Publication Data
Children and stress: understanding and helping / Beverly Hardcastle Stanford and Kaoru Yamamoto, editors.
p. cm.
Includes bibliographical references.
ISBN 0-87173-153-3 (pbk.)
1. Stress in children. 2. Adjustment (Psychology) in children. 3. Stress management. I. Stanford, Beverly Hardcastle, 1938- II. Yamamoto, Kaoru

BF723.S75 C54 2001
155.4'18—dc21 2001041234

Table of Contents

Preface

Alice V. Watkins

In January of 1993, among the many birthday gifts that I received were two books that were so compelling they inspired me to spend hours doing research in the library. I was driven to find evidence that would disprove the truly distressing portrait of life as experienced by millions of children and portrayed in Stephen Shames's *Outside the Dream: Child Poverty in America* and Marian Wright Edelman's *The Measure of Our Success: A Letter to My Children and Yours,* both of which were published in 1991.

The chilling black-and-white images of Shames's photographic essay provided a stark reminder of the neglect of children with special needs in the United States. The data that both Shames and Edelman presented were alarming and prophetic when first written; 10 years later, at the beginning of the 21st century, it is astounding to realize that the conditions for many of the children in the United States and around the world may have deteriorated even further. How do we interrupt the cycle of neglect and destruction that is affecting our most precious resource?

In this book, *Children and Stress: Understanding and Helping,* the authors reach out to those adults who are empowered to nurture, educate, assist, and support children. It is a book for ordinary adults who work and live with ordinary children. It is a book that says, rather simply, that we must redouble our resolve to understand the pressures that children face each day in their homes, schools, and communities. This book declares that children have special needs that must be recognized and attended to by the adults who care for them. Specifically, this is a book that explores the stressful experiences faced by ordinary children every day. The authors present helpful advice and techniques for protecting children during those challenging experiences.

The authors present a case for looking at the lives of all children, and they urge us to renew our commitment to establish environments that eliminate the stress associated with bigotry, school failure, dysfunctional family life, dysfunctional schools, and unsafe communities.

The books written by Stephen Shames and Marian Wright Edelman in 1991 highlighted the millions of children who live in poverty. They also showed how homelessness, divorce, physical abuse, teenage pregnancy, and school dropout further imperil so many of our youngest citizens.

We have begun a new century. Yet, are children less vulnerable today? Are ordinary children, living in stable communities, subjected to a level of stress in their lives that is unparalleled in modern history? The authors of this book suggest that children are indeed subjected to continuing stress at home and in school, and they offer practical suggestions for eliminating the debilitating harm that occurs as a result.

We have a moral obligation to protect our children and provide them with a future that nurtures their imagination, their creativity, and their dreams.

This book is dedicated to the achievement of that goal.

Prologue

The Undefeated: Lessons From Autobiographical Accounts

Marilyn M. Maxson

Reprinted with permission from *The Educational Forum*, Vol. 53, No. 4, Summer 1989.

Several weeks ago a student teacher began telling me about a boy in her classroom who was disliked by the entire class, including the cooperating teacher. The student teacher saw nothing unusual about the child and came to me to ask aid in planning what she might do to help the boy. As she described the child's isolation by both peers and teachers, I began thinking about the days when I was teaching third grade. I, too, once had a student who was rejected by the entire class. The memory made me cringe. Fresh out of teacher preparation, young and idealistic, I had known so little about children's needs and perceptions. Despite my efforts, clumsy as they were, I was unable to help Julia acquire any friends. In fact, I probably made matters worse by allowing the class to confront her in a class meeting over some now forgotten misdemeanor. Unable to guide the class adequately to see that all of us make mistakes, I only succeeded in allowing a deeper wedge to be driven between Julia and her classmates.

Now older and more experienced, I was able to offer my student teacher some advice on how to deal with her class and the boy in question. Still, I wonder what happened to Julia—whether, over the years, she found people who guided her toward better, more healthy ways of relating to others.

While the literature and statistics assure us that many people survive the trials and turmoil of childhood to lead productive, fruitful lives,[1] we who work with children know that there are still too many of them who do not get a chance to fulfill their potential. Some, like the two my student teacher and I worked with, suffer because they do not relate well to others; others, because they lack adequate basic needs like food, clothing, shelter, and/or love; and still others, because they have a physical or mental abnormality. Yet, against these odds we find children who, even when beset by some of life's harshest realities, not only refuse to break, but also make lasting and unique contributions. What helps to build these "self-sufficient, courageous, pragmatic, patient, and compassionate human beings"?[2] "Why do some (few) children survive despite their conditions while others fall prey to them?"[3]

Life From Within

Frankl tells of an elderly doctor who consulted him for severe depression. The doctor could not get over the loss of his wife two years earlier. Frankl asked him:

> "What would have happened, Doctor, if you had died first, and your wife would have had to survive you?" "Oh," he said, "for her this would have been terrible; how she would have suffered!" Whereupon [Frankl] replied, "You see, Doctor, such a suffering has been spared her, and it is you who have spared her this suffering; but now, you have to pay for it by surviving and mourning her." He said no word but shook my hand and calmly left my office.[4]

This episode illustrates that people's perceptions of an experience determine whether they survive and flourish amidst life's trials or wither, becoming angry, embittered, mean, and revengeful. While there is some evidence that our basic perceptions may be somewhat structured from birth, these still appear to be open to influence.[5]

As One Sees It

Janet Frame, the talented Australian writer, tells in her autobiography how John Forrest, a young university instructor in psychology, helped to convince her that she was a schizophrenic. A lonely, sensitive young girl who wanted to write, Frame attempted suicide rather than face a school inspector sent to judge her teaching capabilities. After a six week stay in a mental institution, where she was diagnosed as schizophrenic, she returned to the university town to be near a library. There she felt she could write and read about her "disease without hope," as she termed it. To support herself she took a job attending four elderly, bedridden women in a boarding house. Her only contact with the outside world was her weekly talk with Forrest. As she put it in *An Angel at My Table*:

> My consolation was my "talks" with John Forrest as he was my link with the world I had known, and because I wanted these "talks" to continue, I built up a formidable schizophrenic repertoire: I'd lie on the couch, while young handsome John Forrest, glistening with newly-applied Freud, took note of what I said and did, and suddenly I'd put a glazed look in my eye, as if I were in a dream, and begin to relate a fantasy as if I experienced it as a reality. I'd describe it in detail while John Forrest listened, impressed, serious. Usually I incorporated in the fantasy details of my reading on schizophrenia.
>
> "You are suffering from a loneliness of the inner soul," John said one day. . . . He next made the remark which was to direct my behavior and reason for many years.
>
> "When I think of you," he said, "I think of Van Gogh, of Hugo Wolf. . . ."
>
> . . . once again turning to books for my information, [I] discovered that Hugo Wolf "died insane," and that Van Gogh "shot himself in despair at his condition." I read that Schumann, too, "suffered serious deterioration in mental health." All three were named as schizophrenic, with their artistic ability apparently the pearl of their schizophrenia. Great artists, visionaries. . . .
>
> My place was, then, at the terrible feast. I had no illusions about "greatness" but at least I could endow my work and—when necessary—my life with the mark of my schizophrenia.[6]

Frame, shy, wanting to be liked and well thought of, grasped what possibilities she could to possess her desire—"a place to write, time to write, enough money to live on, somebody to talk to or at least to try to impress."[7] Eventually she actually feared that she was schizophrenic even though she knew that she had not lost touch with reality.

It was years before Frame escaped the schizophrenic diagnosis. Helping doctors because she knew and used the symptoms "when the occasion required," she found herself in and out of mental hospitals for most of her young adult life. Scheduled for a lobotomy, because she had been judged permanently insane, she was saved the night before the operation by the superintendent of the hospital when he heard that her collection of short stories, entitled *The Lagoon*, had won the Hubert Church Award for best prose.

This amazing story underscores how impressionable young people can be. A label applied, even if not rightly so, may lead a person like Frame down a dark and treacherous path.[8] Lacking any evidence from others, the person may opt to believe the label. And, as she points out, put in a situation one grows to learn, and even relish, behaving as she or he is expected to.

The Need for an Other

Knowing that others hold such power over us, providing a framework within which to view our experience, can be at once frightening, as in Janet Frame's case, or reassuring. As other authors have acknowledged, the intervention of one person, at a propitious moment, can change the course of one's life, thus turning a nightmare of survival into a life of creativity and meaning.[9]

D'Ambrosio, in the foreword to his book, *No Language But a Cry*, tells of a young mathematics teacher with steel-rimmed glasses, who spent months tutoring him in fourth- and fifth-grade subjects.[10] D'Ambrosio was placed in a class for the mentally retarded because he had failed to learn to read. His parents, having emigrated from Italy and not speaking English, could not read the correspondence from the school asking them to help him with his reading. If the child had not wandered, by accident, into this young teacher's after-school remedial mathematics class, he would have never left the ghetto, gone on to college, and completed his doctoral studies in psychiatry.

Carl Rowan is another who acknowledges his debt to a particular teacher, a woman who opened his eyes to Shakespeare and encouraged him to be somebody, despite the fact he was born black and deprived.[11] Now a nationally syndicated columnist and roving editor for the *Reader's Digest*, Rowan became the first member of his family to graduate from high school and attend college.

To many others the school and teachers have brought solace in the wake of disaster. Arata Osada recorded the accounts of the children who survived the horror of Hiroshima. Included in these accounts is the story of Sachiko Habu who was five years old at the time of the bombing and wrote about it when she was eleven. The short account cries poignantly of a young girl's love for her dead mother. Yet, beyond the tears lay hope. In Sachiko's words:

> It's already six years since Mother died. When I think that I have not been able to speak to her for all that time it's unbearable, really unbearable. . . . Then every day when I go to school my teacher is kind and teaches me new things, and I play with good friends. I feel happiest going to school.[12]

Teachers have not been the only ones to radically influence a child's life. For Dick Gregory, his mother provided the impetus to overcome poverty and racism to become a track star and, later, a civil rights leader. As he put it in *Nigger*, a loving tribute to his mother's influence:

> Like a lot of Negro kids, we never would have made it without our Momma. When there was no fatback to go with the beans, no socks to go with the shoes, no hope to go with tomorrow, she'd smile and say: "We ain't poor, we're just broke." Poor is a state of mind you never grow out of, but being broke is just a temporary condition. She always had a big smile, even when her legs and feet swelled from high blood pressure and she collapsed across the table with sugar diabetes. You have to smile twenty-four hours a day, Momma would say. If you walk through life showing the aggravation you've gone through, people will feel sorry for you, and they'll never respect you. She taught us that man has two ways out in life—laughing or crying. There's more hope in laughing.[13]

What a person says, the way it is said, and the way one lives can influence children's perceptions of their surroundings, and their life. For Gregory, his "Momma" gave him hope and a glimpse of the way one could face life, live it, and achieve.

The Need for Others

For many children it is not just one person who brings meaning and purpose to life, but several. As Mead argues, safety exists in numbers: "A growing portfolio of attachments provides the newborn with an increased security it would not have if it were dependent for emotional nurturance on only one adult. There is survival value for the child in not 'going for broke' with the mother alone."[14]

In his autobiography, *They Cage the Animals at Night*, Jennings Michael Burch illustrates this point.

From the age of eight until eleven, he spent life in a series of institutions and foster homes because his mother was too sick to care for him and his five brothers. His story is one of repeated misery and physical, as well as emotional, pain at the hands of cruel nuns and vicious foster parents. Yet Burch survived. He survived because, along the way, he encountered peers, a teacher, a bus driver, a cook, a policeman, an older brother, and an understanding nun who gave him a stuffed dog he carried with him everywhere. These people took an interest in him, giving him the love and encouragement he needed to face loneliness, hate, and fear, and to overcome them, even when doing so sometimes caused more pain and hurt.

Near the end of his stay in his last institution, Burch provided another boy with some advice and encouragement to help the child survive his institutionalization. His words encapsulate a part of his story, *They Cage the Animals at Night*:

> I wanted him to at least have a chance at making it. Mark did it for me; it was time I paid him back. . . .
>
> "Listen, Kevin," I said. "You gotta start playing with other kids." . . . "Why?" He blinked his big brown eyes at me. . . . "There's a rule around here that says you gotta play with different kids every day." I avoided his eyes as I spoke. "Do you understand?" "No," he said quietly. . . . "You see, Kevin, if you pal around with only one person all the time and that person leaves, then you're more lonely than before. Understand?" His big eyes welled with tears. "Are you leaving?" he asked. "No, I'm not leaving," I said.
>
> "But that don't matter, Kevin. I'm gonna leave someday and you're gonna have to stay. I want you to have other kids to play with when that happens. Do you understand?" He did. The tears built in his eyes and his lip quivered. A few tears fell, rolling down the comer of his mouth. "Don't cry, Kevin. I'm not saying these things to hurt you." I put my arm around his shoulder. "I'm telling you this stuff to help you."
>
> He got to his feet and looked at me. He wiped his face in one great swipe with the back of his dirty hand. . . . I wanted to hug him, but I didn't. He blinked his eyes and turned around. He started to walk away. I watched him as he walked toward a group of kids. He turned twice to look back at me. I waved my hand for him to keep going. He shuffled along in his baggy pants over to the kids. Kevin was going to make it, I thought. At least he would for now.[15]

Not long after Burch talked with Kevin, a bus driver, who had befriended the lad, came and took him home. Burch made it, unlike one of his brothers who got so used to running away he never stopped, going from one job to another, one place to another, and eventually abandoning a wife and children. But, as Burch notes in his epilogue, it was those special people, many of whom are now memories, who helped him survive.

Reminding Oneself

All children, like Jennings Burch, and the others I have described, need, among other things, charismatic, inspirational people to counter the effects of a disadvantaged background if they are to become competent, well-adjusted, gifted adults. While every case differs from all others, we know that it takes at least one such person who offers love and guidance and provides the child with self-assurance "and a vision of what can be achieved."[16] Each of the people I have described found their person(s) and generated out of chaotic beginnings well-adjusted, creative lives. But there still exist many children from similarly disadvantaged backgrounds and with the same potential talents who are or will be looking for their inspirations.

None of us knows for sure what people, aside from our families, we will influence, or what manner that influence might take. As teachers, however, we need to be aware that we are in a position that allows us potentially to mold a number of children's lives. What we say and how we act toward them may mean the difference between providing them with the courage, hope, and security to flourish and create meaningful, satisfying lives, or consigning them to a life of degradation, insecurity, and unhappiness. The child may be the quiet, shy, soft-spoken girl at the back of the classroom, the rebel down the street who repeatedly has been expelled from school, or the hostile, unhappy urchin on the playground who appears to have no friends—we do not know. Given that, can we afford not to examine our words, actions, and judgments more closely and continuously? That child we ignore, mistreat, or label may have the potential to be another Janet Frame or Dick Gregory. As teachers, we do not want to be remembered for calling a child "backward" as one of Albert Einstein's teachers did.[17] Rather, I believe we would prefer to be remembered as someone who encouraged children to be the best they could be.

Perhaps we can begin by deleting some of the labels we routinely use—poor, hyperactive, broken home, learning disabled, delinquent. Janet Frame's story illustrates how the person may use the label to construct an identity. And, while she was bright and aware when she adopted in her twenties a label to create an identity, not everyone chooses his or her label. Hobbs, among others, warned of what can happen to children labeled delinquent.[18] Marked by the community and peers with suspicion and mistrust, and often isolated within their own families, the "delinquent" children are driven away from the resources they need most to withstand the label, and typically end up molding their behavior to fit the label.

Unfortunately, knowing that labels can have deleterious effects has not deterred our schools in the past 10-15 years from further categorizing and labeling children. Too often these labels carry negative connotations. Sometimes we teachers begin thinking, and perhaps telling, our students of their limitations, rather than reminding them that they are capable, talented, and skillful. Even if the label serves to describe a condition, it never describes the whole child. Maybe, by focusing on what the child can do, we will find, wrapped within the label, an individual of great value to humankind.

As teachers, we need to realize that we serve as potentially powerful role models and, occasionally, inspirations. Do we know, standing before a class, how our words and actions may be interpreted? Too often, I think, we forget, in the daily grind of work, that at least some of our students, in any given moment, are probably watching and listening to everything we do and say. Each word, each action has the possibility of impacting powerfully on one or more of our students. Through our words and actions we can communicate to our students productive and compassionate ways of treating others, coping skills, and ways of achieving. This treatment can lead students to a creative, fulfilling, satisfying life, like Richard D'Ambrosio's or Carl Rowan's. On the other hand, if our words and actions demean, belittle, and disparage, it may stunt and damage a student's life for years (or forever), wasting valuable time and talent, as in the case of Janet Frame. Maybe, the next time we walk into a classroom we should take a moment to collect our thoughts, and remember the potential we have to alter and shape life. Perhaps, the memory will serve to focus our words and actions to match our ideals.

As I look back on the experience with Julia I realize that, had I taken a little more time, sat down and talked with her, and later talked with the class, perhaps I could have helped her open lines of communication with her classmates rather than close them. Had I asked one or two of my more empathic students to make some overt gestures of friendship to Julia, perhaps she would have begun to make friends in the class. I cannot take back those words or actions. But, I can ensure that I do not repeat my past mistakes. Now as I look across my college classroom, before I start to teach a college class, I try to pause long enough to consider: Is what I am about to say or do something I would want students to emulate or model? Will what I do or say harm somebody? Is there a student through a word or gesture I can encourage?

As teachers we cannot be sure whose lives we might touch. We can only hope, through our words and actions, that we will enhance our students' individual dignity and worth, allowing them to make their own unique contributions to humankind. And, perhaps, we will be remembered tomorrow for opening up a child's life as Anne Sullivan did for Helen Keller.

References

The author gratefully acknowledges the comments of Dr. Paul Slayton on an earlier version of this paper.

1. See, for example, E. James Anthony and Bertram J. Cohler, eds., *The Invulnerable Child* (New York: Guilford Press, 1987); Norman Garmezy, "Stress, Competence, and Development," *American Journal of Orthopsychiatry 57* (April 1987): 159-174; Suzanne C. Kobasa, "Stressful Life Events, Personality, and Health: An Inquiry into Hardiness," *Journal of Personality and Social Psychology 37* (January 1979): 1-11; Emmy E. Werner and Ruth S. Smith, *Vulnerable but Invincible: A Longitudinal Study of Resilient Children and Youth* (New York: McGraw-Hill, 1982).
2. Kaoru Yamamoto, *Teaching* (Boston: Houghton-Mifflin, 1969), p. 141.
3. Marilyn M. Maxson, "The World's Children: How Are They Faring?" *The New Era, 60* (No. 5, 1979): 192.
4. Viktor E. Frankl, *Man's Search for Meaning* (New York: Washington Square Press, 1963), pp. 178-179.
5. See, for example, Jerome Kagan, *The Nature of the Child* (New York: Basic Books, 1964); Lois Barclay Murphy and Alice E. Moriarty, *Vulnerability, Coping and Growth: From Infancy to Adolescence* (New Haven, Connecticut: Yale University Press, 1976); Julius Segal and Herbart Yahraes, *A Child's Journey* (New York: McGraw-Hill, 1979).
6. Janet Frame, *An Angel at My Table* (New York: George Braziller, 1984), p. 82.
7. Ibid.
8. For the negative effects of labeling, see Nichols Hobbs, *The Futures of Children* (San Francisco: Jossey-Bass, 1975), particularly Chapter 5, pp. 123-155.
9. See, for example, Wemer and Smith, *Vulnerable but Invincible*; Emmy E. Werner, "Resilient Children," *Young Children 40* (November 1984): 68-72.
10. Richard D'Ambrosio, *No Language But a Cry* (New York: Dell, 1970).
11. Carl T. Rowan, "Unforgettable Miss Bessie," *Reader's Digest 126* (March 1985): 123-126.
12. Arata Osada, *Children of Hiroshima* (Tokyo: Publishing Committee for "Children of Hiroshima," 1980), p. 5.
13. Dick Gregory, *Nigger* (New York: E.P. Dutton, 1964), p. 39.
14. Segal and Yahraes, *Child's Journey*, p. 122.
15. Jennings Michael Burch, *They Cage the Animals at Night* (New York: New American Library, 1984), pp. 217-218.
16. Segal and Yahraes, *Child's Journey*, p. 287.
17. Victor Goertzel and Mildred George Goertzel, *Cradles of Eminence* (Boston: Little, Brown, 1962), p. 248.
18. Hobbs, *Futures of Children*.

Introduction

Beverly Hardcastle Stanford

On the morning of September 11, 2001, just before this book was to go to press, terrorist attacks on the United States took place in New York, Washington, D.C., and Pennsylvania. Americans, young and old, as well as people around the world, watched in disbelief and alarm as television screens repeatedly displayed the horrifying scenes of mass destruction. For too many people, the events would forever change their personal lives, as someone they loved or knew well was killed or injured in the mayhem. Everybody was in shock, vainly trying to understand the unexpected and incomprehensible.

As the adults so reacted, they were closely watched by children, who were frightened, bewildered, and even petrified. As difficult as it was, parents and educators needed to be models of calmness for the children under their care. Many hard questions were to come: "Will we be bombed?" "Why do they hate us so?" "What can we do?" For the sake of the children, the days had to be kept as normal as possible. Adults needed to adapt their responses to children's levels of understanding, taking cues from the children themselves. Numerous acts of heroism, self-sacrifice, and compassion were there in the midst of the disaster and tragedy to serve as uplifting examples for the next generation. And the millions throughout the world who gathered in prayer and candlelight vigils showed children paths of faith and hope.

While the horrors of these events were experienced as a nation and world, the coping and healing will be individual, and the needed skills must have been learned over time for any routine or emergency experience. The task of nurturance and guidance rests with caring adults. We hope that the understandings shared in this book and the advice offered can be of some assistance in that process. The goal of this book is to assist teachers and parents in their efforts to understand and help children.

This book began at a retreat led by Kaoru Yamamoto in a mountain lodge outside Denver. For the second time in several years, a small group of Kaoru Yamamoto's former students gathered from around the United States for a student-initiated, two-day seminar to tap his wisdom on human development and reflect on their own work and lives. Some of us were strangers to each other, having studied with Yamamoto at different times over the previous 30 years. However, our ties to him connected us to each other and promised a kindly mind-stretching time together.

Traveling with me to the retreat was the idea of a book on children and stress, one that would help teachers and others who work with children to better understand and assist children with stress. I was disturbed by the number of my graduate students—novice, mid-career, and veteran teachers—who were stressed themselves by their students' stress. In 20 years of teaching education classes, I had not encountered as many teachers in one year to confide in me that they were overwhelmed by their students' needs and wondered if they could continue to teach. Their helplessness verged on hopelessness, and I worried about them.

Throughout the United States, people responded with similar helplessness to the student violence occurring on school campuses across the United States. Educators, journalists, and psychologists had been writing about the social erosion in America for some years. Using the term "socially toxic" to convey the increasing violence, drugs, family instability, poverty, and meanness permeating U.S. society, psychologist James Garbarino (1995) warned his readers that "as the social environment becomes more toxic, it is the children—particularly the most vulnerable among them—who show the effects first and worst" (p. 6). Journalist Alex Kotlowitz (1991) brought national attention to some of the "most vulnerable" with a book that told, in disturbing detail, the true story of two boys living in a deteriorating Chicago public housing project. When he asked the boys' mother if he could write a book on her children, she agreed and added, "But you know, there are no children here. They've seen too much to be children" (1991, p. x).

During a break at the retreat, I shared my idea for the book with Kaoru and asked if he would co-edit it with me. I was pleased when he agreed and humbled when, with his typical grace and generosity, he insisted that I be the first co-editor. I valued him as an editor when I wrote chapters for two of his earlier books (1978, 1979) and admired his decade-long editorship of *The Educational Forum*, so I knew the project was in good hands. Findings from his series of international studies of children's stress were standard fare in my classes and would be integral content for the book. And his book *Their World, Our World: Reflections on Childhood* (1993) offered the dual perspective I sought for a book on children's stress.

Later, on a short mountain hike during the retreat, I asked Marc Mahlios, a fellow participant, if he wanted to work on the project with us. Marc was a professor in the Department of Teaching and Leadership at the University of Kansas, and had served in key educational leadership positions at several other universities. To my pleasure, he agreed as well. Marc's studies of children's cognitive styles intrigued me, and I looked forward to learning more about the stress that can result from mismatches in teachers' instructional strategies and children's cognitive styles.

A third contributing author, Marilyn Maxson, was with us in spirit only. Marilyn had been especially lively in the previous retreat, challenging us with questions and directives. The following year, she was diagnosed with a brain tumor; weeks before the Denver retreat she died, struck down too soon in an active life and productive career as a university professor, teaching teachers. Kaoru and I decided to re-publish a stress-related article she had written and to use it as our prologue. In that article, she reminds us that adults—especially teachers—have the power to help or harm our impressionable young: "What we say and how we act toward them may mean the difference between providing them with the courage, hope, and security to flourish and create meaningful lives, or consigning them to a life of degradation, insecurity and unhappiness."

The book, thus launched with three authors at the retreat, was like a snowball that grew, picking up contributing authors in the months that followed its trip down the mountain. I enlisted the talents and wisdom of several colleagues from Azusa Pacific University. Maria Pacino provided expertise on cultural diversity, based on her experiences as a professor who teaches courses in multiculturalism, as a Portuguese immigrant who encountered racial discrimination in America, and most important, as a loving mother who empowered her daughter to rise above prejudicial treatment from classmates, neighbors, and even a teacher. Beth Houskamp, a psychology professor, and Rose Huff, a school psychologist, combined their knowledge and experience for our chapter on family-related stress. Special education professor David Colachico accepted the challenge of explaining the stresses affecting children with disabilities and their families. Dan Doorn, a professor who teaches language development classes, drew from his treasury of children's books to recommend relevant titles for several of our chapters, and Marti Villaneuva, a research assistant and caring parent, summarized their contents. Alice Watkins, our dean, kindly agreed to write the preface. In one of her speeches to the faculty, which invariably draw standing ovations, she described children living in poverty as "children without influence or affluence." I wanted her voice in this book.

Gail McEachron, a professor at William and Mary and a valued colleague from earlier writing endeavors, shared her insights on "how stress is manifested in the classroom and how student teachers tend to respond to these socially challenging situations." Sherry Young, a gifted counselor in a private agency in Michigan, gave us a therapist's perspective on children's stress through an instructive glimpse into her therapy practice.

These veteran educators culled from their experience and knowledge the most useful insights and advice they could offer to our intended readers—extremely busy, conscientious educators distressed by their students' stress. Fortunately, the Association for Childhood Education International and its chief editor, Anne Bauer, were similarly concerned about children and stress, and they supported our effort.

The resulting book explores children's ordinary stress—such as the embarrassment of being chosen last for a team, the hurt of being left out of a clique, and the humiliation of not being able to grasp a concept that classmates find easy. While these stresses may pass, from a child's perspective they are "always and forever." The shock and pain of being called names because of one's skin color, the helplessness when parents divorce, the anger that results from being bullied, and the hopelessness after repeated failures are even heavier loads frequently carried into adulthood.

The authors believe that adults, especially parents and educators, can assist and advocate for today's children. We need only locate our place on the spectrum of awareness-to-understanding-to-action and proceed forward. Accordingly, the structure of this book reflects that continuum. Each chapter contains illustrative cases to assist with awareness, theory and research to increase understanding, and suggested courses and resources to consider for taking action.

Part I of the book explores children's experiences with and perceptions of stress, focusing on the areas of family, culture, school, and children with special needs. It begins with an inside view of children's stress and offers approaches for successful adaptation. A premise throughout the book is the authors' belief that life for a child is not as easy as adults like to think. Indeed, too often in our world today, it is hard to be a child.

Part II looks at the professionals who work with children—the teacher educator, student teacher, veteran teacher, and therapist—and considers how they can alleviate children's stress. To recognize the importance of caring for the caregivers, one section pays attention to adults' stress. Our focus on professionals is not intended to minimize the much more significant influence of parents. That important discussion would require another book, however.

Unfortunately, some situations that seem hopeless to children, seem hopeless to adults as well. Nevertheless, adults—individually and working together—can overcome such challenges and reduce social toxins and their impact on children's worlds. As this book was being prepared, several hate crimes occurred in my community. In reaction, "nearly 80 residents turned out [to a community meeting] to wage war on the criminals who [had] been intimidating them and their children" (Rester, October 31, 2000, p. A1). Someone at the meeting described past problems in another violence-prone neighborhood in town, where children went to school crying because "gang members would tell them they [would be] lucky if their moms were alive when they came home." Using building code violations and the legal system to pressure apartment owners to clean up or close down, the city succeeded in having the neglected complex vacated and torn down. A community response by adults—residents, parents, city officials, and police—made the difference then and continues to do so today.

When stressful events cannot be changed or avoided, we need to know how to help children as they pass through the hard times. In the following pages, our contributors—educators, therapists, and psychologists—offer insights, options, and resources for that worthy endeavor. That these offerings will lighten the loads of children and the adults who watch over them is our greatest hope.

Endnote

We are indebted to Deborah Byrnes and Gary Kiger for the structural model they provide in their useful book *Common Bonds: Anti-Bias Teaching in a Diverse Society* (1996) (also published by the Association for Childhood Education International). I am also grateful to Azusa Pacific University for granting me a Provost's Grant to work on this book and related projects.

References

Garbarino, James. (1995). *Raising children in a socially toxic environment.* San Francisco: Jossey-Bass.

Kotlowitz, Alex. (1991). *There are no children here.* New York: Doubleday.

Rester, Michelle. (October 31, 2000). Residents meet city officials on safety. *San Gabriel Valley (CA) Tribune*, pp. A1, A5.

Yamamoto, Kaoru. (Ed.). (1978). *Death in the life of children.* West Lafayette, IN: Kappa Delta Pi.

Yamamoto, Kaoru. (Ed.). (1979). *Children in time and space.* New York: Teachers College Press.

Yamamoto, Kaoru. (1993). *Their world, our world: Reflections on childhood.* Westport, CT: Praeger.

PART I

Stress: Children's Experiences

Chapter 1
Stress: The View From the Inside

Kaoru Yamamoto

What worries me a lot is my mom . . . ah, she went on a boat . . . and then the boat sounded way far away and then she never came back. That worries me a lot.

This terse remark made by a 4 and 1/2-year-old boy hides the depth of his emotion associated with the experience so briefly sketched. (We were visiting with several young children to talk about things that make us feel sad, worried, upset, or angry [Dibrell & Yamamoto, 1988].) Visualize, if you will, a child standing on a windswept seaside hilltop to watch a gray naval vessel slowly sailing off, *with his mommy on it*, to an unknown destination. The boy does not fully understand the "why" or the "how-long" of her voyage. At the breakwater, heading for the vast, blue horizon, the ship sounds its deep horn—ever so forlorn a farewell. Feeling very funny in his tummy, the child tightens his grip on his granny's hand, and she reciprocates. As comforting as her grasp is, it is *not* that of Mommy's. Many questions run through his mind: Did I do something so bad as to make her angry and go away? Can she see me now—crying, waving, sorry, and scared? Will she forgive me and come back someday? Oh, please, please, God!

The Notion of Stress

Although the word *stress* is used routinely in everyday conversation, the physiological and psychological concept has a rather short history. A medical researcher named Hans Selye (who was born in Vienna in 1907 and died in Canada in 1982) borrowed the idea and terminology from material science. In that field, a material (e.g., metal, concrete, or rope) can be subjected to some external force (or "stress") by hitting, pressing, pulling, or swinging it. What transpires within the material in reaction to that stress is called the "strain." If the force used is strong enough, and/or sustained long enough, the material will ultimately show "fatigue" and eventually "fail" from the strain.

Unfortunately, when Selye adopted the idea to use in the realm of health sciences, he, by his own admission, mistakenly applied the word *stress* to what should have been *strain*, or the reaction to stress. As a result, he later found it necessary to coin a new word, "stressor" (Selye, 1978, pp. 50-51), to refer to "that which produces stress" (p. 78). Therefore, in the medical (and still later, psychological) literature, stressors bring forth stress within an organism.

Selye discovered that, irrespective of the particular nature of the stressor and the particular part or system of the body it initially affects, the overall pattern of the organism's reaction to injuries, diseases, and other stressors is nonspecific. Selye used common hormonal responses as evidence, but it is now acknowledged that "the component which is common . . . appears to be some aspect of emotional arousal" (Levine, 1988, p. 109), which then leads to the shared physiological phenomenon. In any case, the organismic reaction follows a sequence through three phases: 1) alarm, 2) resistance, and 3) exhaustion. In first encountering stressors, the body reveals certain, generalized physiological changes, such as a considerable enlargement of the adrenals, an intense atrophy of the thymus and lymph nodes, ulcers in the intestinal tract, a loss of weight, and a disarrangement of body temperature.

This initial phase, which serves to alert the organism, is followed by the resistance phase, which mobilizes the organism against the damage brought on by stressors. Unfortunately, "after still more prolonged exposure . . . this acquired adaptation [is] eventually lost" leading to the final phase of exhaustion (Selye, 1978, pp. 37-38).

The "General Adaptation Syndrome (GAS)" or biological stress syndrome, as described above, is "not specific, since it can be produced by virtually any agent." Because of that, "stress cannot and should not be avoided" in daily experiences (Selye, 1978, p. 63). However, some stress, called "distress," would be more unpleasant and harmful than the second variety, known as "eustress." The latter adds color and flavor to life, so to speak, thus providing the necessary tension and the welcome sense of excitement and exhilaration. "The fact that eustress causes much less damage than distress graphically demonstrates that it is 'how you take it' that determines, ultimately, whether one can adapt successfully to change" (Selye, p. 74).

The Common Threads

In considering the psychological aspects of stress, therefore, we need to be aware of both what is common to children in general and what is unique to a given child. Each defines and clarifies the other, since individual differences can be understood only against the overall commonalties, while consistencies can be seen only across variations.

Selye believes that each person is born with a fixed amount of "adaptation energy" as genetic givens. While some people may have more than others, the total for any person is finite. How the individual expends that energy will make a difference in the style and duration of life itself. This whole process may be better described in a slightly more elaborate way than the single "reservoir" analogy. Think of a shallow well that must naturally be replenished by groundwater from time to time. Here, what is limited is not only the total water reserve in the ground, but also the immediately available supply at any one time. The water in the well itself could be exhausted in short time if lavishly used. Even when reasonably husbanded, the well can dry up under heavy or prolonged demand. When the water in the well has thus been drained, no additional supply may be rapidly obtained. Therefore, the maximum capacity *per se* of the water reserve is not the sole predictor of the life of the well.

In other words, the effects of a stressor on anyone depend upon several factors that *interact* with each other. They include: 1) the intensity of the stressor, 2) the duration of the stressor, 3) the person's state of being (i.e., the coping capacity), and 4) the circumstances of the experience (Torrance, 1965). As can be readily inferred, the impact of a severe stressor could be extensive even if its duration were brief. A sudden loss of somebody close to oneself, for example, leaves most people in shock, and the effects are usually devastating as well as long-standing. Likewise, an unexpected accident, injury, or financial setback represents a real tribulation for most people.

On the other hand, even a stressor of lesser intensity may become quite destructive if it were protracted long enough so as to chip away at a person's adaptive potential. An unhappy home wherein parents constantly quarrel, fight, and scheme against each other, or where they repeat a cycle of angry walkouts and dubious rapprochements, would be much less tolerable than an open breakup in which the parents are "careful not to divorce themselves from their children" (Grollman, 1972, p. 235). In another example, the effect of protracted stress may be understood through the Chinese communists' successful utilization of "psychological crowding." Unlike their contemporaries in Russia, the Chinese communists did not use isolation and physical torture as the central means for changing the minds of their political and military prisoners. Instead, they depended heavily upon the "manipulation of privacy"; the highly crowded prison cells made it "impossible to escape from one's fellows, even for an instant" (Frank, 1974, p. 93). Whether in prison, project housing, or a classroom, incessant and noise-filled group life without any time or place for solitude, privacy, and silence will take a toll.

As will be further discussed later in this book, one's capacity for handling stress hinges upon many closely interwoven factors of nature *and* nurture. The full utilization of any coping potential, however, may depend heavily upon the person's action or inaction at the very onset of the stressful experience (Torrance, 1965). It is typically difficult in the early moments to recognize clearly the nature of the stressor and the enormity of the possible or actual damage. The 1912 *Titanic* incident remains a classic example. Even the seasoned seafarers underestimated or ignored the gravity of that situation, and failed to mobilize quickly enough for a maximum effort that critical. The tragic results are well known.

Of course, it does not take a calamity of that magnitude to remind us how important an early and total response to a challenge can be. A child who does not, or cannot, finish the drudgery of tying shoelaces before running full speed out of the house is likely to come quickly to grief!

The tendency to overlook or ignore signs of trouble, and thus remain inactive, often proves to be the major determinant of the damage magnitude in disasters of all sorts, whether natural or man-made. It is not that the common initial reactions of disbelief, denial, despair, and grief are totally without merit. In fact, they serve to protect the person from the danger of rapid disintegration, and allow time for proper mobilization for the crisis. The problem, rather, is that too long a sojourn in the overwhelming, incomprehensible present tends to prevent one from moving in all due speed into reconstructive and preventive actions.

An unfortunate case in point is the many children whose lives have been marred by the delay *on the part of adults* in noticing and handling early indications of psychomotor, cognitive, and/or affective difficulties and damage. While the youngsters themselves may not clearly recognize the nature of their afflictions, they will suffer from cumulative negative effects of such conditions. As time goes by without suitable restorative measures or developmental guidance, children who are behind or astray at the outset may face an increasing burden of recuperation. Even intensive remedial efforts may prove progressively ineffective under such circumstances.[1]

To recapitulate, the effects on a given person of any stressor rarely can be explained by the features of the stressor itself, the characteristics of the individual alone, or the contexts of the experience *per se.* All factors enter into the picture in interaction, and each factor functions as a mediator for others. This becomes quite clear when we consider the circumstances for any particular event in life. For instance, during the Second World War, about 825,000 English school children were evacuated (without their parents) from the major cities under incessant German air attacks to protect them from the horrors of destruction, injury, and death (see, e.g., Wicks, 1989). Of those who were removed to rural safety, it was estimated that a quarter to one half showed neurotic symptoms. In clear contrast, those who remained in the cities with their families during the Blitz exhibited fewer such difficulties. On the unevacuated group of children, Anna Freud and Dorothy Burlingham (1943) had this to say:

> General sympathy has been aroused by the idea that little children, all innocently, should thus come into close contact with the horrors of the war. . . . [However,] so far as we can notice there were no signs of traumatic shock to be observed in these children. If these bombing incidents occur when small children are in the care either of their own mothers or a familiar mother substitute, they do not seem to be particularly affected by them. . . . It is a widely different matter when children, during an experience of this kind, are separated from and even lose their parents. (pp. 20-21)

Given the "secure base" of the family (Bowlby, 1988) for support, the record shows that the seemingly vulnerable young ones not only survived the harrowing days and nights, but also prevailed against all the unmentionable terror, want, and misery by using some of the best weapons in their own arsenal—play and humor, imagination and hope (see, e.g., Rosenblatt, 1984; Westall, 1987). Indeed, to repeat Selye (1978), "it is 'how you take it' that determines, ultimately, whether one can adapt successfully to change" (p. 74).

The View From Within

How a person responds to stress has much to do with that person's view of "reality." We know that each child constructs a unique reality out of her or his experiences in the course of developing within a particular cultural milieu (Piaget, 1973). Since the elements, both material and nonmaterial, that constitute the child's experience are mostly shared within a given social-ecological setting, those growing up in a common environment are likely to create similar realities. That is the reason why members of a particular group feel they can understand each other, while often having difficulty in *reading* those from outside the group—that is to say, a different culture.

It is important to remember, however, that even within a shared culture, each person's reality is in essence one of a kind. This point was made seven decades ago by the sociologists William and Dorothy Thomas (1928), who wrote that, "If men define situations as real, they are real in their consequences" (p. 572). In other words, the constructed reality (i.e., what is perceived to be real and construed to be true) is what largely orients an individual's thoughts and feelings, and guides her or his actions. The view of the world seen from inside a person's life context is singular, and it seldom coincides perfectly with the outside-in views of others. For mutual understanding and nurturance, therefore, it is critical for each, as an individual and as a group, to learn and appreciate other, differing realities.

What, then, are the realities of young children? As regards their perceptions of events that upset them, our own studies have allowed us a glimpse of *their* world in contrast to *ours* (Yamamoto, 1993). By approaching youngsters, from preschoolers through 9th-graders, and asking them to rate each of 20 potentially stressful experiences on a scale ranging from 7 (the most upsetting) to 1 (the least), and to report on their own trials and tribulations, we have learned some worthwhile lessons. The children who have taken part in this research now number close to 4,000, and they are from such diverse places as the United States, Canada, Iceland, the United Kingdom, South Africa, Egypt, Japan, the Philippines, and Australia (see, Yamamoto, Davis, Dylak, Whittaker, Marsh, & van der Westhuizen, 1996; Yamamoto, Soliman, Parsons, & Davis, 1987).[2]

The findings were quite uniform essentially everywhere. The responses varied little in relation to the children's gender or grade, or to whether they actually had undergone the particular experiences. To our initial surprise, the ordering of the life events in terms of their mean "upsettingness" ratings remained amazingly similar across the world, as seen in the sample listings in Table 1.

Within the United States, the correlation coefficients across the 20 events among the differing groups of children were 0.95-0.98, regardless of the locale of study, the age of children, or the ethnic composition. The results from other lands were correlating 0.80-0.98 with the U.S. findings, with a median of 0.92, and 0.70-0.97 among themselves, with a median of 0.88.[3] Thus, the agreement was remarkable among youngsters who had never heard of each other, much less mingled together.

Of course, within each group of children, a certain dispersion of opinions could be found, but it was uniformly the case that the more stressful an event was rated, the less variation there was in the ratings. The reported incidences of these experiences were also very much alike, the correlations ranging from 0.98 to 0.51, with the median of 0.85.

TABLE 1
CHILDREN'S RATINGS ON STRESSFULNESS OF LIFE EVENTS*

Life Events	Children's Groups†								
	US(a)	US(b)	US(c)	US(d)	Egypt	Japan	S.Africa	UK	Iceland
Losing my mother or father	6.90	6.85	4.90	4.94	6.88	6.90	6.92	6.91	6.95
Going blind	6.86	6.68	4.93	4.82	6.83	6.68	6.76	6.85	6.90
Being kept in the same grade next year	6.82	6.67	4.80	4.57	6.83	6.78	6.43	5.71	6.41
Wetting pants in class	6.74	6.45	4.77	4.70	6.73	6.73	6.47	5.95	6.69
Hearing my parents quarrel and fight	6.71	6.60	4.76	4.75	6.83	6.23	6.64	6.57	6.51
Being caught stealing something	6.63	5.87	4.78	4.75	6.62	6.73	6.25	6.03	6.74
Telling the truth, but no one believing me	6.53	5.78	4.56	3.85	6.62	6.73	6.15	5.13	5.97
Receiving a poor report card	6.23	6.00	4.77	4.53	6.69	6.61	5.37	4.99	4.65
Being sent to the principal's office	5.75	4.32	4.80	4.76	6.63	6.63	5.67	4.96	3.89
Going to a hospital for an operation	5.51	4.45	4.69	4.71	6.55	5.82	5.15	5.02	5.47
Getting lost in a strange place	5.49	4.41	4.80	4.77	6.52	5.01	5.00	4.61	5.55
Being laughed at in front of the class	5.28	5.15	4.36	4.20	6.63	6.11	5.05	4.62	5.81
Moving to a new school	4.60	4.27	3.67	2.58	6.52	5.21	4.12	3.70	4.19
Having a scary dream	4.08	3.67	4.35	4.31	6.59	5.07	5.45	4.00	6.23
Not making a perfect score (100) on a test	3.75	3.75	3.80	3.16	6.46	5.04	5.71	4.50	2.23
Being picked last on a team	3.30	3.53	3.00	2.83	4.73	5.92	3.77	2.77	3.40
Losing in any game/sports	3.16	2.73	2.68	2.79	5.68	4.48	2.56	2.06	2.16
Going to a dentist	2.73	1.84	1.40	1.26	4.87	3.05	1.95	1.31	2.31
Getting up in front of the class to give a report	2.58	2.38	1.89	1.46	3.08	2.75	1.92	1.98	2.77
Having a new baby sister or brother	1.27	1.31	1.07	1.66	1.20	1.43	1.26	1.23	1.23
Number	367	170	108	270	296	248	295	366	244
Grade	4-6	6	3	1	3-6	4-6	3-8	3-6	4-9

*The scale value is the median of the ratings, ranging from 7 (the most upsetting) to 1 (the least upsetting) for all groups except US(c) and US(d). For these two groups of younger respondents, the scale was curtailed to five, rather than seven, points. [When standardized, the scores on the longer and shorter scales correlated 0.82 to 0.93 with each other with a median of 0.90.]

†The mean ratings in this table are excerpts from Yamamoto, Soliman, Parsons, and Davis (1987), Yamamoto and Byrnes (1987), and Yamamoto, Davis, Dylak, Whittaker, Marsh, and van der Westhuizen (1996).

On the event list, "Losing my mother or father" is rated the most upsetting by everyone, closely followed by "Going blind." Such responses appear quite commonsensical, yet the realities underlying the children's responses may not be so simple. For example, the loss of parent does not necessarily mean his or her demise. A child can lose a parent in many different ways, and the core experience of loss itself is the source of stress, regardless of the specific form a particular loss may take. Such a loss could be a result of separation, divorce, desertion, sickness, and so on. Indeed, much more routine and common situations, such as unintended neglect due to a parent's chronic illness or preoccupation with work, may rival or even surpass the negative effect of a parent's dramatic physical departure. Subtle parental rejection of a child is yet another common form of loss.

As a matter of fact, one encounters in print and visual media quite a few reports on the troubled life of the young (e.g., Elkind, 1981; "Kids Growing," 1994; "Little Big People," 1993; Louv, 1992; Miller, 1983; Postman, 1982; "Through the Eyes," 1988; Weissbourd, 1996; Winn, 1984). One common thread in most such portrayals is the sense that the parent has somehow ceased to be a parent, breaching or renouncing his or her responsibilities in relation to a child or children. The overall impression is that feelings of devastation and emptiness are rather pervasive among many young people (as well as among the not-so-young ones!) who *perceive* a major loss, under one guise or another, in the relationship with their parents.

Alas, even well-intentioned parents may never know the trouble children see, unless they remain tuned to the "view from within" of thc young.[4] In the inimitable words of Antoine de Saint-Exupéry (1971),

> "Only the children know what they are looking for," said the little prince. "They waste their time over a rag doll and it becomes very important to them; and if anybody takes it away from them, they cry. . . ." "Now here is my secret, a very simple secret: It is only with the heart that one can see rightly; what is essential is invisible to the eye." (pp. 89 & 87)

Needless to say, the challenge to see with the heart applies to all kinds of life events, and not merely to the most trying experiences. An example we came across in talking with preschool and kindergarten children was the remarkably uniform image of the hospital (Dibrell & Yamamoto, 1988). Not surprisingly, the children felt sad, scared, or simply bad about going to the hospital, but what epitomized this institution in their minds was not the imposing buildings, not the doctors and nurses in white or green uniforms, not the people in beds covered also in white, and not the mysterious machines of all sorts. Rather, they said they were afraid of "shots"! When asked what made them feel better in the face of the dreaded injections, many mentioned Band-aids because, in the authoritative words of one little boy, "Band-aids heal!" Candy, gum, balloons, and toys were also mentioned frequently as alleviating measures. Obviously, the children considered these items to be serious remedies, not mere gimmicky tinsels.

Storms of Life

As indicated by our studies, only partially summarized in Table 1, experiences that tend to bother and upset children may be conveniently clustered into two groups. The first of these has to do with the child's sense of security, reflected in such events as the loss of parent, loss of sight, parental fights, and getting lost. The sensed threat can be physical and/or mental, and it derives from a basic anxiety about being isolated, abandoned, and/or helpless. Fromm (1970) aptly notes that: "While insofar as he [*Homo sapiens*] is an animal he is most afraid of dying, insofar as he is a man he is most afraid of being utterly alone" (p. 104). In the course of development, a child's fundamental sense of security hinges upon the reliable availability of benign, caregiving adults, especially parents. Hence, to most children, "hearing [one's] parents quarrel and fight" understandably would be a seriously unsettling experience. Likewise, such events as "getting lost in some strange place" and "moving to a new school" often place the child through the ordeal of being totally alone.

The second cluster of stressful experiences is related to the child's sense of honor and dignity. For instance, "telling the truth, but no one believing me" is an event rated pretty high in upsettingness (the median being ca. 6.00 on the 7-point scale), and reported to have been actually experienced by a large majority of children (the median proportion is about 83 percent). In contrast, the median experiential proportion was only about 15 percent for "being caught stealing something," although its median stress rating was even higher at ca. 6.20.

Anything that is denigrating, shaming, and embarrassing is upsetting to the child. "Wetting pants in class," "Receiving a poor report card," "Being sent to the principal's office," or "Being laughed at in front of the class" all belong in this cluster. So also does the experience of academic retainment, an event that, in most countries, was rated third, following only the loss of a parent and the loss of sight. The practice of holding a pupil in the same grade for an extra year varied widely in its reported frequency (3.6 to 47.5 percent) in different countries, but its capacity to cause upset was rated uniformly high, the median being 6.31. Such findings serve as a good reminder that, regardless of the advisability of a given child-rearing or schooling practice, its application must be done carefully so as to prevent disgracing and wounding children. "The one sin that is unforgivable is to diminish a student's sense of dignity and worth" (Wigginton, 1986, p. 235).

To sum up, the young are apprehensive of being left isolated, powerless, and helpless. Like grownups, they wish to have a basic sense of safety and security in life, which should not be governed by chaos, arbitrariness, or malevolence. Children would like to be able to foresee, at least to some degree, the future course of events. Therefore, they wish to be reasonably autonomous and feel somewhat in control of their own lives. Just as adults do, children want to be respected by their fellows. For all its fragility, their sense of honor and integrity is of no less import to the soundness of their being than it is in the "bigger people."

The effective functioning of a person hinges upon how well she or he handles unavoidable pressures, conflicts, and frustrations in life. Such adaptive efforts may be understood to operate at three levels: 1) defense, 2) coping, and 3) mastery.

What have been called the mechanisms of defense constitute the first tier, including such processes as displacement, rationalization, projection, suppression, repression, regression, identification, compensation, reaction formation, and sublimation. Perhaps due to their original identification by Sigmund Freud on the basis of his work with "neurotic" patients, most of these mechanisms often have been viewed in a somewhat unfavorable light. However, they do serve the valuable purpose of defending oneself against hurt, guilt, anxiety, and disintegration. Therefore, they can be helpful devices in handling stress, and there is nothing inherently abnormal or shameful about them. Indeed, "active coping efforts often go hand in hand with defense mechanisms, [which are] temporarily useful" (Murphy & Moriarty, 1976, p. 345).

Nevertheless, because such defense is typically an automatic reaction under a sensed imminent threat, many of these responses carry a somewhat desperate, fight-or-flight flavor. As a result, they tend to be rather blindly applied to any and all situations, irrespective of timeliness or appropriateness. When applied in such a rigid, indiscriminate manner, useful and usually protective efforts can end up harmful. So-called "accident prone" or "bad luck" people, who seem to suffer from repeated mishaps or relational failures, may be reflecting unconscious patterns of reaction, rather than fate or destiny.

In contrast, when we speak of the second tier of adaptation (namely, coping), the intentional element in the selection of approach(es) become more apparent. Rather than a knee-jerk response that is characteristic of defense, what emerges is a more conscious, problem-solving orientation. "We see children confront new situations and challenges calling for responses not previously crystallized" (Murphy et al., 1962, p. 6). The child develops ways of dealing with trying conditions and tasks, depending on the nature of the specific stressors, the particular circumstances, and the internal and external resources at hand. "Defense mechanisms may be, and often are, part of the overall coping effort; they sometimes assist in dividing a complex situation into manageable parts, through repressing the excessive threat and focusing on the one that can be" more readily handled (Murphy et al., 1962, p. 7). Thus, dividing and conquering is frequently effective not only in war, politics, and sports, but also in coping for adaptation.

What needs to be remembered is that no single and uniform set of coping devices may be prescribed for all. Simple forgetting, evasion, avoidance, or postponement might allow children the time to regroup before wrestling with some challenges under certain circumstances. Crying, reasonable expression of anger, vigorous physical exertion, or fantasies could serve cathartic purposes. Once strong emotions have been released, the situation may be better assessed and possible approaches more lucidly formulated. Then, a frank confrontation with the task and an all-out effort may bring forth an acceptable resolution.

Even in quite unbearable situations (such as living in bomb-devastated cities under the threat of constant air raids), many children have managed to prevail by changing the trying experience into a game or contest of some kind (e.g., Westall, 1987). Other children, caught in heavy crossfire between two battling armies, prayed and sang to allay their fears and keep up their courage (e.g., Roth-Hano, 1989). Humor also has been a useful way to transform a harrowing or awkward experience into something manageable. Diversion of one sort or another can be not only a device for brief escape and recuperation, but also a means of changing one's outlook and, hence, restructuring the situation (i.e., one's reality). In many instances, working with and through others can bring better results than a solo attempt can. Ironically, but not surprisingly, children's *play* contains numerous effective tactics for dealing with significant threats to one's stability and functioning (Yamamoto, 1977).

Finally, at the third tier of successful adaptation, we speak of mastery. Indeed, all the coping efforts are motivated by the quest for mastery. "The process of mastery . . . involves the parallel and successive use of different devices and resources, according to the cognitive, affective, and motor levels of integration in response to each new challenge" (Murphy et al., 1962, p. 162). Obviously, the experience does not follow a smooth, linear, developmental progression, uniform for all children. In fact, it has been observed that the "flexible use of defense mechanisms were [*sic*] part of coping" (Murphy & Moriarty, 1976, p. 337), and "the most effective children, the best copers if you like, allowed themselves leeway for regression" (p. 345).

Thus, the pursuit of mastery is a perennial effort—two steps forward, one step back. "Coping techniques and styles evolve and change over time" (Murphy & Moriarty, 1976, p. 338), while "the best copers among boys and girls [are] those with the widest range of coping resources" (p. 337), including both active and passive devices. Each challenge that is handled successfully through a child's autonomous efforts adds to that child's self-confidence, pleasure, and sense of worth, but "some loss of their best functioning [should be expected to occur] in all children in the face of one or another experience evidently felt as threatening or stressful" (Murphy & Moriarty, 1976, p. 346). Mastery is a lifelong process, not a lifetime status.

The Helping Hands

In listening to children, one cannot help being touched by the profound sense of vulnerability among them. They remain fundamentally dependent upon adults for a long time, afraid of abandonment, apprehensive of what lies ahead, and uncertain of what they can do. Surrounded by many upsetting encounters and unpredictable events, they harbor hurt feelings and imagine dire possibilities, whether realistic or not. The intricate contingencies of life may be too much for their budding cognitive structures to accommodate, and strong, complex emotions can be too threatening to handle. Still, they, like everyone else, must somehow make sense of their own worlds. Too often, children must persevere and persist in the face of the unknown and the overwhelming.

Adults can, and must, render vital assistance by providing an anchor. Suitable explanations of experienced and anticipated events, coupled with acceptance and clarification of attendant feelings, provide a backdrop of security. Against a steady background of close child-adult relationships, built over time through countless small, but significant, daily interactions of a sensitive nature, children will develop and "play out" their specific schemes of understanding and coping. It is instructive to read, out of a massive study based upon longitudinal observations of children's daily activities from infancy on (Murphy & Moriarty, 1976), that "the parents of good copers neither indulged their children nor overprotected them. They respected their children's capacities, encouraged and rewarded their efforts, and offered reassurance in times of frustration and failure" (p. 349). This whole orientation must become a daily way of life at home and in school, since we grow in life mainly by living it today, even as we prepare for tomorrow.

Children and adults are better off if they are prepared, both emotionally and intellectually, for what might be coming their way. Such preparation does not have to be overly detailed. Rather, the emphasis should be on giving a child a general idea of the experience, what it is about and like, and providing her or him with a few essentials about what and how to do—or not to do. That sort of "advance organizers" knowledge (Ausubel, 1968) goes a long way in preventing the child from feeling utterly lost and powerless when an actual distressful event occurs. His or her coping mobilization should be much quicker and more appropriate because of that preparation. Adults can assure children that everyone would be a bit scared, nervous, sad, or lonely in an unfamiliar territory (i.e., a new experience), and that they should not be afraid of such feelings or be ashamed of crying or getting mad a little.

Discussing and practicing with children some concrete things to do in the face of a stressful situation can serve them in even common daily circumstances of potential or real danger—when lost in a large store, when hurt riding a bike, when a stranger beckons in a park or from a car, when trapped in an elevator, when the electricity goes out, when a fire starts somewhere in the school, when a classmate is suddenly stricken with illness, etc. Such actions may be simple, but will give a child something familiar and definite to do, and they help focus children's minds on the task at hand rather than on the trying experience. As long as the child can do something, no matter how limited, she or he feels more the master of fate than its slave; consequently, that sense of self-control works against fright, panic, and chaos.

Clearly, no "crisis" reactions or "emergency" measures will be effective when dealing with future disasters, unless the child receives sustained nurturance and guidance in everyday coping efforts. While studies have not so far unraveled any simple, single answer to the mystery of the origin of competence, invulnerability, or resilience against the storms of life, some experiences and arrangements in the personal background may in fact work as protective factors to buffer or reduce the negative effects of stressors, while others (vulnerability factors) may aggravate such effects. Examples of protective factors would be family, classroom, or community climates of support, stability, and cohesion. According to Rutter (1988, p. 24), "Good personal relationships and social supports may mitigate the effects of stressful life events, and . . . a lack of such intimate relationships increase the adverse effects of stressors." Garmezy (1987) adds that children with greater "assets," such as higher intelligence, higher socioeconomic class, and family attributes of stability and cohesion, appear to be more competent and, when under pressure, less disruptive in the classroom and better socially engaged with their peers.

Meanwhile, Werner and Smith (1989) pointed to three clusters of factors that may account for the "vulnerable but invincible" children they had followed for more than three decades: 1) positive disposition of the child (active, good-natured, responsive, autonomous, etc.) and adequate intellectual and communication skills; 2) supportive family environment (smaller family size, close parent-child relationship, family caregivers in addition to the mother, clear household structure and rules, a sense of family cohesion, etc.); and 3) external ties with the wider community (close peers, supportive neighbors and elders, trusting and trusted teachers/coaches/ministers, access to social services, etc.). These observations are in close agreement with the findings from another study of resilient children successfully raised in an economically troubled, rural environment (Elder, Conger, Parke, & Elder, 2000). Werner further noted that, "Most resilient individuals who had coped successfully with adversity in childhood and adolescence are also competent in coping with their adult responsibilities" in their early 30s (1989, p. 78).

Because "the risks to which children are exposed are as variable in their severity and nature as the vulnerabilities and resiliences with which the children confront them" (Anthony, 1987, p. 10), it is extremely difficult to predict the developmental outcomes of individuals. Nevertheless, a solid foundation laid early in life by the parents, teachers, and other concerned adults adds to the protective factors of any child.

> [Children] need adults who do something obvious in conception but rare in reality: who actually listen to them and see them clearly and who understand how their lives are affected by their families, schools, and communities. It is out of such clear visions that we can make childhood gratifying and help children develop the strengths and trust they'll need as adults for productive work, enthusiastic friendship, and lasting love. (Weissbourd, 1996, p. 237)

This is our opportunity, and this is our responsibility. Are we adult enough to take up the challenge? That is *the* question.

Endnotes

1. An extreme situation may be found in the condition of infantile autism. While the precise dynamics of this "profound aloneness" (a phrase coined by Leo Kanner, a pioneer in child psychiatry, whose work paralleled that of Hans Asperger's) still remains opaque, the suffering of the afflicted youngsters and their parents is all too real. See, for example, Frith, 1991; Happe, 1998; Rayment, 2000.
2. Some additional details of the findings may be found in separate articles on Iceland, Japan, the Philippines, South Africa, the United Kingdom, and the United States. For the exact sources, kindly contact the author.
3. The sole, interesting exception was found in Poland. However, even the seemingly divergent results from this Eastern European land made sense when its societal dynamics were more closely examined. See Yamamoto, Davis, Dylak et al., 1996.
4. One of our recent studies offers hope in relation to this quality of parental "tuning" to the inside-out view of children. See Yamamoto and Mahlios, 2001.

References

Anthony, E. James. (1987). Risk, vulnerability, and resilience: An overview. In E. James Anthony & Bertram J. Cohler (Eds.), *The invulnerable child* (pp. 3-48). New York: Guilford Press.

Ausubel, David P. (1968). *Educational psychology: A cognitive view.* New York: Holt, Rinehart & Winston.

Bowlby, John. (1988). *A secure base.* New York: Basic Books.

Dibrell, Lorraine L., & Yamamoto, Kaoru. (1988). In their own words: Concerns of young children. *Child Psychiatry and Human Development, 19,* 3-25.

Elder, Glen H., Conger, Rand D., Parke, Ross D., & Elder, Glen H., Jr. (2000). *Children of the land: Adversity and success in rural America.* Chicago: University of Chicago Press.

Elkind, David. (1981). *The hurried child.* Reading, MA: Addison-Wesley.

Frank, Jerome D. (1974). *Persuasion and healing.* New York: Schocken.

Freud, Anna, & Burlingham, Dorothy T. (1943). *War and children.* London: Medical War Books.
Frith, Uta. (Ed.). (1991). *Autism and Asperger syndrome.* New York: Cambridge University Press.
Fromm, Erich. (1970). Psychoanalysis and Zen Buddhism. In Erich Fromm, D. T. Suzuki, & Richard de Martino (Eds.), *Zen Buddhism and psychoanalysis* (pp. 77-141). New York: Harper Colophon Books.
Garmezy, Norman. (1987). Stress, competence, and development. *American Journal of Orthopsychiatry, 57,* 159-174.
Grollman, Earl A. (Ed.). (1972). *Explaining divorce to children.* Boston: Beacon Press.
Happe, Francesca. (1998). *Autism.* Cambridge, MA: Harvard University Press.
Kids growing up scared. (1994, January 10). *Newsweek,* pp. 42-50.
Levine, Seymour. (1988). A psychobiological approach to the ontogeny of coping. In Norman Garmezy and Michael Rutter (Eds.), *Stress, coping, and development in children* (pp. 107-131). Baltimore: Johns Hopkins University Press.
Little big people. (1993, October 10). *The New York Times Magazine,* pp. 28-34.
Louv, Richard. (1992). *Children's future.* New York: Anchor Book, Doubleday.
Miller, Alice. (1983). *The drama of the gifted child.* New York: Basic Books.
Murphy, Lois Barclay, & Associates. (1962). *The widening world of childhood.* New York: Basic Books.
Murphy, Lois Barclay, & Moriarty, Alice E. (1976). *Vulnerability, coping, and growth.* New Haven, CT: Yale University Press.
Piaget, Jean. (1973). *The child and reality.* New York: Viking Press.
Postman, Neil. (1982). *The disappearance of childhood.* New York: Dell.
Rayment, Tim. (2000, June 18). In a lonely place. *The Sunday Times Magazine* (London), pp. 28-36.
Rosenblatt, Roger. (1984). *Children of war.* Garden City, NY: Anchor Press, Doubleday.
Rutter, Michael. (1988). Stress, coping, and development: Some issues and some questions. In Norman Garmezy & Michael Rutter (Eds.), *Stress, coping, and development in children* (pp. 1-41). Baltimore: Johns Hopkins University Press.
Saint-Exupéry, Antoine de. (1971). *The little prince.* New York: Harcourt Brace Jovanovich.
Selye, Hans. (1978). *The stress of life* (Rev. ed.). New York: McGraw-Hill.
Thomas, William I., & Thomas, Dorothy S. (1928). *The child in America.* New York: Alfred A. Knopf.
Through the eyes of children. (1988, August 8). *Time,* pp. 32-57.
Torrance, E. Paul. (1965). *Constructive behavior.* Belmont, CA: Wadsworth.
Weissbourd, Richard. (1996). *The vulnerable child.* Reading, MA: Addison-Wesley.
Werner, Emmy E. (1989). High-risk children in young adulthood: A longitudinal study from birth to 32 years. *American Journal of Orthopsychiatry, 59,* 72-81.
Werner, Emmy E., & Smith, Ruth S. (1989). *Vulnerable but invincible.* New York: Adams, Bannister, Cox.
Westall, Robert. (1987). *Children of the Blitz.* Hammondsworth, Middlesex, England: Penguin Books.
Wicks, Ben. (1989). *No time to wave goodbye.* New York: St. Martin's Press.
Wigginton, Eliot. (1986). *Sometimes a shining moment.* Garden City, NY: Anchor Press, Doubleday.
Winn, Marie. (1984). *Children without childhood.* New York: Penguin Books.
Yamamoto, Kaoru. (1977). Humankind: Shadows and images. In Louise M. Berman & Jessie A. Roderick (Eds.), *Feeling, valuing, and the art of growing* (pp. 11-28). Washington, DC: Association for Supervision and Curriculum Development.
Yamamoto, Kaoru. (1993). *Their world, our world.* Westport, CT: Praeger.
Yamamoto, Kaoru, & Byrnes, Deborah A. (1987). Primary children's ratings of the stressfulness of experiences. *Journal of Research in Childhood Education, 2,* 117-121.
Yamamoto, Kaoru, Davis, O. L., Jr., Dylak, Stanislaw, Whittaker, Jean, Marsh, Colin, & van der Westhuizen, P. C. (1996). Across six nations: Stressful events in the lives of children. *Child Psychiatry and Human Development, 26,* 139-150.
Yamamoto, Kaoru, & Mahlios, Marc C. (2001). Home is where it begins: Parents, children, and stressful events. *Journal of Child Psychology and Psychiatry, 42,* 533-537.
Yamamoto, Kaoru, Soliman, Abdalla, Parsons, James, & Davis, O. L., Jr. (1987). Voices in unison: Stressful events in the lives of children in six countries. *Journal of Child Psychology and Psychiatry, 28,* 855-864.

Further Sample Resources

General Discussion of Stress

Adler, Jerry. (1999, June 14). How stress attacks you. *Newsweek*, pp. 56-63.

Tanner, Ogden. (1976). *Stress.* New York: Time-Life Books.

The Experience of Being a Child

[An overview for parents and teachers]

Klein, Carol. (1975). *How it feels to be a child.* New York: Harper Colophon Books.

LeShan, Eda J. (1971). *The conspiracy against childhood.* New York: Atheneum.

Uslander, Arlene, Weiss, Caroline, Telman, Judith, & Wernick, Esona. (1974). *Their universe.* New York: Delta Book, Dell.

Waksler, Frances Chaput. (1996). *The little trials of childhood and children's strategies for dealing with them.* London: The Falmer Press.

Yamamoto, Kaoru. (Ed.). (1972). *The child and his image.* Boston: Houghton Mifflin.

Yamamoto, Kaoru. (Ed.). (1979). *Children in time and space.* New York: Teachers College Press.

Yamamoto, Kaoru. (1993). *Their world, our world: Reflections on childhood.* Westport, CT: Praeger.

Young, Leontine. (1966). *The life among the giants.* New York: McGraw-Hill.

[Providing help by using oral and written stories, "What if" situations, club and group activities, etc.]

Fassler, Joan. (1980). *Helping children cope.* Riverside, NJ: The Free Press.

Humphrey, Sandra McLeod. (1995). *If you had to choose, what would you do?* Amherst, NY: Prometheus Books.

Livo, Norma. (1994). *Who's afraid . . . ?: Facing children's fears with folktales.* Englewood, CO: Teacher Ideas Press, Libraries Unlimited.

Makins, Virginia. (1997). *The invisible children: Nipping failure in the bud.* London: David Fulton.

Loss and Death in Childhood

[Loss of parent]

Davidman, Lynn. (2000). *Motherloss.* Berkeley, CA: University of California Press.

Furman, Erna. (1974). *A child's parent dies.* New Haven, CT: Yale University Press.

Grollman, Earl A. (1967). *Explaining death to children.* Boston: Beacon Press.

Grollman, Earl A. (1970). *Talking about death.* Boston: Beacon Press. (A conversational explanation with a child.)

Knowles, Don, & Reeves, Nancy. (1983). *But won't Granny need her socks?: Dealing effectively with children's concerns about death and dying.* Dubuque, IA: Kendall/Hunt, 1983. *(Includes workshop-derived exercises and guidelines for caregivers.)*

LeShan, Eda. (1976). *Learning to say good-by.* New York: Macmillan.

Ross, Jim, & Myers, Paul. (Eds.). (1996). *Dear Oklahoma City, get well soon.* New York: Walker. (Outpourings of children's sentiments after the April 19, 1995 bombing.)

Ward, Barbara, & Associates. (1993). *Good grief: Exploring feelings, loss and death with under elevens.* London: Jessica Kingsley.

Yamamoto, Kaoru. (Ed.). (1978). *Death in the life of children.* West Lafayette, IN: Kappa Delta Pi Press.

[Stricken Child]

Bertoia, Judi. (1993). *Drawings from a dying child.* London: Routledge.

Bluebond-Langner, Myra. (1978). *The private worlds of dying children.* Princeton, NJ: Princeton University Press.

Bombeck, Erma. (1989). *I want to grow hair, I want to grow up, I want to go to Boise.* New York: Harper & Row.

Kirps, David L. (1989). *Learning by heart: AIDS and school children in America's communities.* New Brunswick, NJ: Rutgers University Press.

****

[The following titles were written by or for children.]

Gaes, Jason. (1987). *My book for kids with cansur.* Aberdeen, SD: Melius & Peterson.

Sanford, Doris. (1989). *In our neighborhood, David has AIDS.* Portland, OR: Multnomah.

Swain, Jonathan, & Schilling, Sharon. (1989). *"My name is Jonathan (and I have AIDS)."* Denver, CO: Prickly Pair.

[Loss of Child]
Finkbeiner, Ann K. (1996). *After the death of a child: Living with loss through the years.* Baltimore: Johns Hopkins University Press.
Kübler-Ross, Elizabeth. (1983). *On children and death.* New York: Macmillan.
Oyler, Chris. (1988). *Go toward the light.* New York: Harper & Row.
Schiff, Harriet Sarnoff. (1977). *The bereaved parent.* New York: Crown.

Bullying
Hazler, Richard J. (1996). *Breaking the cycle of violence: Interventions for bullying and victimization.* Washington, DC: Accelerated Development.
Ross, Dorothea. (1996). *Childhood bullying and teasing: What school personnel, other professionals and parents can do.* Alexandria, VA: American Counseling Association.

Taxonomic Review of Research
Honig, Alice Sterling. (1986a). Stress and coping in children (part 1). *Young Children, 42(May)*, 50-63.
Honig, Alice Sterling. (1986b). Stress and coping in children (part 2). *Young Children, 42 (July)*, 47-59.

Chapter 2
The Impact of Family Stress Upon School-Age Children

Beth M. Houskamp and Rose Huff

Stressors that affect families can be temporary, such as having a new baby in the home or moving to a new neighborhood. Children who are particularly sensitive to these experiences may become quite distressed and their emotional reactions may affect their experience at school. Other stressors affecting families are more severe and chronic in nature—poverty, for instance. Children who have been forced to cope with and adapt to such circumstances over a long period of time may have very different "stress reactions." Some children frequently witness violence or are themselves victims of violent and abusive behavior. These kinds of experiences shape children's emotional reactions in yet other ways. Finally, some children experience the chronic illness of a parent and/or the death of that parent.

Because the average child spends a significant amount of time with his or her elementary school teacher, these teachers cannot help but become aware of how stress that originates at home (here, "family stress") can affect a child. Eventually, the impact of stress will manifest itself in classroom behavior. The classroom teacher, then, often is in the best position to know when children need help. This chapter will explore how different stressors affect elementary school students, provide case examples, and include a brief discussion of how teachers can determine if a consultation or referral to a mental health professional would be helpful.

Temporary Stressors of Adjustment

Stephanie is a bright and sensitive 7-year-old. While she is an excellent student and understands concepts quickly, she gets frustrated and cries easily when trying new things, her feelings are easily hurt, and she has difficulty staying calm and emotionally stable. Because of her oversensitivity, she has difficulty making friends. In the last two months, Stephanie appears even more agitated, needs all of the teacher's attention, and has at least one major emotional "meltdown" every day at school. In frustration, the teacher calls in Stephanie's parents for a conference. They willingly agree to come in and arrive at the meeting with their 3-month-old baby boy. Over the din of the baby's screams, the parents explain that the boy has very bad colic and screams every day from late afternoon until evening. The parents are aware that Stephanie is sensitive to, and quite distressed by, the baby's crying. It is difficult for the entire family. In fact, they took the boy along because they felt they could not leave him with a sitter, due to the intensity of his cries and the level of stress it tends to produce in others.

In Stephanie's case, the particular stressor causing her problems was very obvious (the birth of a new brother and his colic), was likely to be relatively short-term (colic is usually not a chronic condition), and would not likely create a long-term behavior problem for Stephanie. Once the teacher understood the source of the problem, that Stephanie was being forced to cope with a significant amount of change and chaos at home, she realized that Stephanie would need more support from her for a time.

Stephanie's situation was likely to be only for the short term. Other short-term stressors that might produce noticeable behavioral changes at school include the temporary absence or illness of a parent, or the family moving from one home to another. These stresses generally are manageable for most children and do not usually place a child at risk for psychiatric problems (Rutter, 1996).

Coping, Risk Factors, and Resiliency

A number of factors in a child's life can either help the child cope more easily with stressful situations or hinder a child from adjusting well. The child's temperament is a very important factor (Greenspan, 1998). Some children are naturally easygoing even at a young age; other children, such as Stephanie, tend to be more emotionally reactive, aggressive, or introverted. Depending on temperament, each child will respond to family stress differently. Children who are naturally easygoing and flexible have some built-in protection from stress. In addition, children may gain protection from severe stressful reactions if they have good friends, and if they are flexible and possess good coping skills. Children also may be less vulnerable to family stress when relatives live nearby and thus can offer help in any family emergency, when the family has adequate financial resources, and when the child has outlets for sufficient recreation.

Some children appear to have certain risk factors that leave them vulnerable to stressful situations (Cicchetti & Toth, 1998). These risk factors may contribute to, although not necessarily be predictors of, future problems. Such factors can include anxiety, depression, a history of abuse or neglect, having multiple caregivers without a solid attachment figure (for example, children who spend a significant amount of time in foster care), poverty, overcrowded home conditions, and parents who commit crimes (Cicchetti & Toth, 1998; Mash & Barkley, 1996; Rutter, 1985). Both internal characteristics (such as a child's temperament) and external stressors (such as a high degree of conflict in a family) could further affect a child who is already vulnerable. So, a 4th-grader who was born with a more difficult temperament, who comes from a high-conflict family with inadequate financial resources, and who is living in cramped quarters has a number of risk factors that could predispose him toward emotional problems.

On the other hand, researchers in child development have shown that, aside from some emotional distress, significant family stressors do not always adversely affect children's development. Certain traits protect children, including high intelligence, an easygoing and flexible temperament, good social skills, positive peer relationships, close relationships with adults other than parents, and good problem-solving skills (Cicchetti & Toth, 1998; Mash & Barkley, 1996). Consequently, a teacher may not realize that the bright, cheerful, and easygoing 4th-grader's mother has just been divorced for the third time, the family's income has just been significantly reduced, and that the child misses her seldom-seen biological dad very much. Stressors that might upend one child may be negotiable for another one.

Divorce

Casey is a 4th-grader who likes math and sports. In the middle of the previous summer, his parents began the process of marital separation and his father moved out of the house. Divorce proceedings began in the early fall of that year, and now Casey is shuttled between two homes. Although he had struggled with organizing his homework and class materials, Casey had been an average student up to that point. Since his parents began the divorce proceedings, however, Casey has not been completing assignments or turning in all his homework. His teacher arranges a parent-teacher conference to discuss his conduct. Casey's parents are shocked to discover that he is often inattentive, forgetful, and irritable in class. Although the teacher had sent home several notes regarding her concerns about Casey, none of them reached Casey's parents. As his parents begin to fire recriminations at each other, Casey simply grows more sullen and upset.

Children today are more and more likely to have parents who are divorcing and remarrying. According to the most recent U.S. Census Bureau figures, over one million children experience divorce each year (cited in Amato & Keith, 1991). Most of the research assessing the effect of divorce on kids (e.g., Amato, 1994) suggests that a stress model can best reflect the complexity of divorce and children's reactions. The impact of divorce upon children seems to depend upon the severity of such factors as the economic well-being of the custodial parent, how the custodial parent handles the divorce, the level to which the noncustodial parent becomes absent from the child's life, and the level of conflict between the divorcing parents. In addition, divorce can precipitate other stressful events for the child, such as remarriage of one or both parents and a move to a new household and/or neighborhood (Amato, 1994).

The divorce process may trigger in children certain telltale signs of stress. In particular, teachers may see more disruptive behavior in class, including noncompliance, aggression, and impulsiveness (Wallerstein, 1987). School-age children whose parents are going through divorce may be struggling to sort through their grief and feelings of loss (Wallerstein, 1987). These symptoms obviously can affect children's ability to function well at school; they may have difficulty sharing or playing cooperatively with others, or may act more aggressively. Some children may become more withdrawn, anxious, or sad. Younger children may show some regressive behavior, such as wetting their beds at night or wetting their pants at school, sucking their thumbs, or using babyish speech. These behaviors indicate that the child is having some difficulty adjusting to a new situation, and that he or she may need extra emotional support for a time. The more difficult the family situation is and the less able the family is to emotionally support the child, the more likely it is that the child will exhibit some emotional adjustment problems (King, 1992).

It is important to note, furthermore, that divorce is not an isolated event. Rather, divorce is one step in a process of transitions for all of the family members (Brody & Neubaum, 1996). The family has likely been in turmoil for a long time before the divorce proceedings began, and the family probably will have to renegotiate all sorts of decisions for years to come. More than one half of divorced mothers remarry, and so many children spend at least part of their lives with stepfamilies (Brody & Neubaum, 1996). In addition, the rates of redivorce are also quite high; many children may live in several stepfamily situations throughout their childhood, and so must make the adjustment to new family members several times.

Long-term behavior problems in the classroom are often a sign that the family stress includes not just the fact of the divorce itself, but also the entire divorce process. If the parents are fighting over custody or having difficulty disciplining their children, the child may be caught in the middle. When parents have been divorced and remarried several times, the stress becomes chronic. If the custodial parent's income is significantly diminished by the divorce and the child has had to change his or her home, school, and general lifestyle as a result, he or she may exhibit more behavioral problems (Brody & Neubaum, 1996).

Poverty

Jana is a quiet student who loves to read and to help with classroom chores. Her teacher notices, however, that Jana often misses three or four consecutive days of school at the end of each month. She also notes that Jana is sometimes drowsy and listless by midmorning. On several occasions, Jana comes to school wearing clothes that are noticeably dirty, and she carries a foul personal odor. Some of the other students tease her about her appearance and odor, and most students will not play with her. Jana plays alone, reads, or helps the teacher. At times, her teacher sends her to the school nurse to wash and change clothes. At lunch, Jana pockets packaged food items. Her teacher attempts to set up a parent-teacher conference, but finds this difficult to do as Jana's family does not have a telephone. Also, her parents work only intermittently—when and where they can find employment.

When a parent-teacher meeting finally takes place, the teacher learns that the family has little food by the end of each month, and has even lived in their car when funds are especially scarce. As they do not always have hot water, showers and clean clothes are, at times, a luxury they cannot afford. Jana is alone with her two siblings some evenings when her parents work, or are looking for work, and her ever-present sense of fear prevents Jana from sleeping soundly. Toward the end of the month, before federal financial assistance arrives, Jana is particularly hungry, dirty, and tired.

Unfortunately, many elementary school students experience chronic, long-term stress related to living in poverty. Researchers have documented an increase in the official rate of childhood poverty within the past several decades. As of 1993, 22.7 percent of children in the United States under age 18 were classified as poor, and 38 percent of all Americans classified as poor were children. Poverty primarily affects ethnic minority children, with rates of poverty being significantly higher among Native American, African American, and certain subgroups of Latino and Asian children, compared to Caucasian children (U.S. Bureau of the Census, 1994).

As Jana's case illustrates, children living in poverty often have to overcome significant hurdles simply to get to school in the morning. They may lack appropriate shelter or supervision, for example. They may not be able to acquire school supplies, keep track of library books, or find a quiet corner at home in which to complete homework assignments. Their parents must struggle to find food and shelter, and therefore often have little time or energy to offer their children.

Poverty also spawns a host of other problems that can have a major influence on children's emotions, behavior, and ability to learn. Poverty is highly associated with homelessness, street violence, and illegal drugs (McLoyd, 1998). Children living in poverty often are malnourished, which over time can impede a child's ability to learn and can contribute to social withdrawal, delayed physical growth, and delayed motor development. Malnourished children score much lower on tests of vocabulary, reading comprehension, arithmetic, and general knowledge (Brown & Pollitt, 1996). These learning and behavior problems can continue even after a child is enrolled in public school and starts receiving free or reduced-price breakfast and lunch at school.

Poverty is a complex stressor. Nancy Guerra (1995) examined three factors that were hypothesized to increase risk for aggression among urban children: economic disadvantage, stressful events, and individual beliefs. She found that being poor was not as much of a contributor to increasing aggressive behavior in these urban children as were their beliefs about violence and their exposure to stressful events. Simply living in poor communities, however, means that these children are more likely to experience stressful events such as witnessing violent or aggressive behavior.

Attachment Problems

Lizbeth is a 6-year-old kindergartner attending local public school. She currently lives with her maternal grandmother, who is her legal guardian. Her mother was abusing drugs and a neighbor reported her to the Department of Children's Services for child neglect. Lizbeth's mom would leave her alone for nights at a time, fail to provide adequate meals, and send her to live with various relatives. Lizbeth was without any permanent residence. Lizbeth's father has been in prison since Lizbeth was a baby. In the classroom, Lizbeth does not listen to instructions, gets into fights with other kids, and acts defiant when the teacher attempts to discipline her. Recently, Lizbeth was very excited when she came to school because her grandmother had bought her a bed. She had never had her own bed before.

In the past three decades, teachers are seeing more and more children like Lizbeth in their classrooms. The increased availability of drugs has taken a toll upon families. Children of drug-addicted parents sometimes end up living on the streets, with grandparents, or in foster care. These children do not experience consistency from adults, do not trust that adults have their best interests at heart, and do not understand loving discipline. Many children, such as Lizbeth, suffer from emotional neglect and long-term relationship or attachment problems.

Researchers who have studied the long-term effects of lack of attachment in early childhood (Ainsworth, 1982; Bowlby, 1969; Greenspan, 1998) explain that children have basic needs that must be met in order to be emotionally and intellectually healthy. These basic needs are: a safe, secure, and nurturing environment that includes a daily relationship with at least one stable, predictable, comforting, and protective adult; emotional interactions geared to the child's developmental needs and level; ongoing, intense relationships with the same caregivers, including the primary one, early in life and throughout childhood; experiences that build a sense of initiative and competency, including those that allow for risk-taking and failure; clearly determined and communicated limits, expectations, structure, and boundaries; and stable neighborhoods and communities within which families can achieve these goals (Greenspan, 1998).

Attachment theorists emphasize that all of these needs center around a solid attachment to a primary caregiver who is emotionally and intellectually available to the child from an early age onward. In the above case study, Lizbeth did not receive consistent caregiving, and so did not develop a sense of trust and did not learn social skills within the context of a consistent, caring relationship. Furthermore, Lizbeth did not receive much intellectual stimulation. Her mother was not available to read nightly bedtime stories, for example; whatever money was available went to buy drugs, not books or intellectually stimulating toys. Lizbeth's community was unstable and dangerous: drug dealers sold their wares on the corner where the school bus stopped and violent crime was prevalent. Although children who, like Lizbeth, have attachment problems present significant challenges for already overburdened teachers, interaction with a caring adult can be significantly helpful.

Greenspan and Salmon (1996) recommend "floor-time" for children who lack consistent, nurturing adults in their lives. During floor time a caring adult (parent, teacher, or other significant person) sits down with the child for 20 minutes or so, several times a week. The goal is to make a concerted effort to connect emotionally with the child through participation in some activity that the child enjoys—playing a game, doing a puzzle, playing with Legos, or reading a book together, for instance. Although it is impossible for teachers to offer such attention to every child in class, children who have not had a solid attachment relationship in their lives desperately need such focused interaction. In the classroom setting, parent volunteers could help provide such stable relationships. As the child and adult spend more time together, the child benefits from an increased ability to regulate herself, calm herself, and act in socially appropriate ways in the classroom.

Pressures on Time and Autonomy

Jenny is a 4th-grader attending an exclusive private school for girls. She is an only child. Both of her parents have very successful careers and work long days—her mother is a lawyer and her father is a heart surgeon. Her parents take turns giving Jenny breakfast and dropping her off at school at 7 a.m. when the early arrival child care begins. After school, Jenny often has a scheduled activity such as piano lessons, swim team, or soccer. She is picked up from school each afternoon by a high school senior who drives her to the scheduled activity, drives her home, cooks her dinner, helps her with homework, and gets her ready for bed. One of Jenny's parents strives to get home before 8:30 p.m. to say goodnight to Jenny before she falls asleep. On the weekends, Jenny spends part of Saturday at a dance class and Sunday morning at church activities. Jenny, always a bright, cheerful, and emotionally responsive child in the past, is now having daily temper tantrums at school and at home with the babysitter. She is increasingly isolated, has trouble turning in schoolwork on time, and is angry and defiant.

Counselors and educators are observing an increasing number of attachment and other related problems in young children from middle and upper socioeconomic groups. Many children from financially middle- or upper-class familes spend a significant amount of time away from home each day, and they also, as early as preschool and elementary school, bear a great deal of pressure to succeed. Teachers who teach in financially well-off neighborhood schools or in private schools are increasingly working with children whose time is rigorously scheduled from morning until evening. These children have little time to enjoy activities at home with a parent. In response to the lack of attention and emotional attachment in their home, some children become overtly angry. Other increasingly common problems reported by children in such high achievement-oriented settings include anxiety, tension, muscle aches, gastrointestinal problems, and high blood pressure. Children whose lives are highly scheduled also benefit from one-on-one time with a caring adult. Floor time (Greenspan, 1998) that is specifically focused on emotionally connecting in a cooperative activity is helpful for these children.

CHILD MALTREATMENT

Although Daniel is a capable student, he has difficulty sitting still in class. He is often given negative reinforcement (such as recess detention or a visit to the principal's office) to redirect him toward appropriate behaviors, both in and out of the classroom. He makes frequent, unwanted physical contact with other students. Daniel has a quick temper and tends to view others' motives as hostile, even when interactions are friendly. He is quick to verbally put down other students, and has been disciplined for laughing when others are hurt. When the school counselor talks to Daniel alone, she discovers a very frightened and insecure side to him. He reveals graphic details of bystanders being gunned down in his neighborhood. The counselor is struck by his accounts of such events as common and, in particular, by his lack of emotion as he speaks. Daniel wants more than anything else to learn karate so that he can protect his family from his alcoholic father. His expression becomes wide-eyed when he speaks of his father coming home from work, and of how difficult it is to determine his father's mood. As Daniel sees it, detecting his father's mood helps him anticipate what kind of evening the family will endure and enables him to find the best way to keep his brother out of his father's way. If his father has been drinking and the kids get in the way, Daniel knows they will be hit hard.

Child maltreatment can be categorized into four general types: physical maltreatment to the point of some bodily injury; sexual contact, or attempted sexual contact between an adult and a child; failure to provide minimum care or appropriate supervision; and neglect of a child's basic emotional needs. Research in this area suggests that many children experience more than one type of maltreatment at the same time (Cicchetti & Toth, 1998). Because of the amount and quality of time teachers spend with children in their classes, teachers are often one of the first adults outside of a family to realize that a child may be experiencing maltreatment.

Seriously maltreated children often struggle to reach basic developmental milestones—cognitive as well as emotional milestones. These children may act aggressively towards others (or, conversely, live in excessive fear of others) and disrupt others through temper tantrums and other outbursts. In addition, these children often have difficulty finding empathy or developing a sense of right and wrong (Cicchetti & Toth, 1998).

Several additional aspects of child maltreatment are worth noting. First, attachment theory provides an effective framework for understanding abused children's experiences (Cicchetti & Toth, 1995). A loving, stable bond with a caretaker often can serve as a protective factor that can minimize the emotional damage brought on by maltreatment. A trauma model also is useful in understanding the effects of maltreatment on children. Research on Post-Traumatic Stress Disorder (PTSD) describes the debilitating effects that may follow a terrifying event. Often, people with PTSD have persistent, frightening memories of their ordeal, which leave them emotionally numb, especially with people they were once close to. War veterans first brought PTSD, once referred to as shell shock or battle fatigue, to public attention, but it can result from any number of traumatic incidents: witnessing domestic or gang violence, being involved in serious accidents such as car or train wrecks, or being the victim of chronic physical or sexual abuse. The symptoms of PTSD are generally similar in children and adults. After a traumatic experience, a child may be subject to recurrent or intrusive recollections, including repetitive play, frightening dreams, or reenactment. The child tries to avoid the thoughts, feelings, people, and places associated with the traumatic event, and so may be unable to recall important aspects. There also may be signs of general emotional numbing, a diminished interest in life, and a sense of hopeless or doubt about the future (Cohen, Berliner, & Mannarino, 2000).

Children suffering from PTSD symptoms often act very angrily and aggressively with teachers and friends. They may entertain thoughts of suicide, they are often very depressed, and they have a high rate of psychiatric hospitalization. Sexually inappropriate behavior and conduct disorders (lying, stealing, truancy) are more common in children who have been severely abused. Traumatized children are more likely than others to need remedial classes and are more likely to be suspended from school. These children often have difficulty getting through a day without experiencing emotional distress. She may be the angry child who is constantly picking fights with others. He may be the quiet child who sits in the corner and never turns in any work. Ultimately, these children have little emotional energy left to devote to their schoolwork. The daily task of survival uses up most of their resources.

Signs That Family Stress May Be Overwhelming a Child

Some degree of occasional family stress is a part of life; grandparents and other older relatives die, parents take new jobs, families move, and babies are born. Families are dynamic, changing entities. When changes occur, most children can cope quite well. A child's ability to cope, however, depends greatly upon having an emotionally stable family that provides a caring and consistent presence. Only then can children devote their full attention to learning. An inability to adjust to a family stressor will manifest itself in two areas: their functioning at school and their ability to maintain friendships.

Teachers are often the first ones to realize that a child is not functioning well in his or her daily environment. An emotionally connected and caring teacher can become the "safe port in a storm" for children who are experiencing family stress. Such teachers are conscious of little things, such as greeting by name each child at the classroom door in the morning and noting the child's mood. For children who do not receive much emotional support or praise at home, one good word from a teacher will provide the emotional support to help them get through the day. For children experiencing a short-term family stress, an extra moment or two of an adult's time will help strengthen their emotional coping skills. Even for children experiencing extreme family stress (such as child abuse or a family member's drug problems), the benefits of a kind word from the teacher or aide, and a few extra moments of the teacher's time, cannot be underestimated.

Sometimes, however, a child is simply not emotionally up to the task of learning new material. When a teacher believes that family stress is significantly affecting a child, additional support may be necessary. That support will vary, depending upon the school setting, the family's stressor, and the financial resources available. A common option is a consultation with the school psychologist, who can offer support, assess the students, and recommend that the child or family attend therapy. Teachers also can make referrals to a community counseling clinic, a parenting class, or a child therapist in private practice.

Although a school counselor or private therapist can be a tremendous resource for the teacher, it is likely that the teacher will spend significantly more time with the child each week than anyone else and thus can provide a unique perspective on the child's behavior and interactions with peers and adults.

Therefore, a therapist should work closely with the teacher. Teachers have the opportunity, in these cases, to change not only the child's academic experience, but also his life experience. For these children, spending 6 hours a day with a caring, emotionally connected adult is a significant gift.

References

Ainsworth, Mary. (1982). Attachment: Retrospect and prospect. In C. Parkes & J. Stevenson-Hinde (Eds.), *The place of attachment in human behavior.* London: Tavistock.

Amato, Paul R. (1994). Life-span adjustment of children to their parents' divorce. *The Future of Children: Children and Divorce, 4*(1),

Amato, Paul R., & Keith, B. (1991). Parental divorce and the well-being of children: A meta analysis. *Psychological Bulletin, 100,* 26-46.

Bowlby, John. (1969). *Attachment and loss: Vol. 1. Atttachment.* New York: Basic Books.

Brody, Gene H., & Neubaum, Eileen. (1996). Family transitions as stressors in children and adolescents. In C. Pfeffer (Ed.), *Severe stress and mental disturbance in children* (pp. 559-590). Washington, DC: American Psychiatric Press.

Brown, J. Larry, & Pollitt, Ernesto. (1996). Malnutrition, poverty and intellectual development. *Scientific American, 274*(2), 38-43.

Cicchetti, Dante, & Toth, Sheree L. (1995). Child maltreatment and attachment organization: Implications for intervention. In S. Goldberg, R. Muir, & J. Kerr (Eds.), *Attachment theory: Social, developmental, and clnical perspectives* (pp. 279-308). Hillsdale, NJ: Analytic Press.

Cicchetti, Dante, & Toth, Sheree L. (1998). Perspectives on research and practice in developmental psychopathology. In I. Sigel & K. A. Renninger (Eds.), *Handbook of child psychology* (5th ed., pp. 479-584). New York: John Wiley & Sons.

Cohen, Judith A., Berliner, Lucy A., & Mannarino, Anthony P. (2000). Treating traumatized children: A research review and synthesis. *Trauma, Violence, and Abuse: A Review Journal, 1*(1), 29-46.

Greenspan, Stanley I., & Salmon, Jacqueline. (1996). *The challenging child: Understanding, raising, and enjoying the five "difficult" types of children.* New York: Perseus Press.

Greenspan, Stanley. (1998). *The growth of the mind: And the endangered origins of intelligence.* Reading, MA: Perseus Publishing.

Guerra, Nancy G. (1995). Stressful events and individual beliefs as correlates of economic disadvantage and aggression among urban children. *Journal of Consulting and Clinical Psychology, 63*(4), 518-528.

King, H. Elizabeth. (1992). The reactions of children to divorce. In C. E. Walker & M. C. Roberts (Eds.), *Handbook of clinical child psychology* (2nd ed., pp. 1009-1023). New York: John Wiley & Sons.

Mash, Eric J., & Barkley, Russell A. (1996). Child psychopathology: A developmental-systems perspective. In R. A. Barkley & E. J. Mash (Eds.), *Child psychopathology* (pp. 3-62). New York: Guilford Publications.

McLoyd, Bonnie. (1998). Children in poverty: Development, public policy, and practice. In I. Sigel & K. A. Renninger (Eds.), *Handbook of child psychology* (5th ed., pp. 135-208). New York: John Wiley & Sons.

Rutter, Michael. (1985). Resilience in the face of adversity: Protective factors and resistance to psychiatric disorder. *British Journal of Psychiatry, 128,* 493-509.

Rutter, Michael. (1996). Transitions and turning points in developmental psychopathology: As applied to the age span between childhood and mid-adulthood. *International Journal of Behavioral Development, 19,* 603-626.

U.S. Bureau of the Census. (1994). *Statistical abstract of the United States: 1994.* Washington, DC: U.S. Government Printing Office.

Wallerstein, Jill. (1987). Children of divorce: Report of a ten-year follow-up of early latency age children. *American Journal of Orthopsychiatry, 57,* 199-211.

Additional References for Teachers

Bowlby, John. (2000). *Attachment* (Basic Books Classics) (2nd ed.). New York: Basic Books.

Brazelton, T. Berry, & Greenspan, Stanley I. (2000). *The irreducible needs of children: What every child must have to grow, learn, and flourish.* Reading, MA: Perseus Books.

Cicchetti, Dante, Rappaport, Julian, Weissberg, Roger P., & Sandler, Irwin N. (Eds.). (2000). *The promotion of wellness in children and adolescents.* CWLA Press.

Greenspan, Stanley I., & Salmon, Jacqueline. (1996). *The challenging child: Understanding, raising, and enjoying the five "difficult" types of children.* New York: Perseus Press.

James, Beverly. (1994). *Handbook for treatment of attachment-trauma problems in children.* New York: The Free Press.

Resources for Children

Armstrong, William H. (1989). *Sounder.* HarperCollins. Addresses: Poverty. For ages 9-12.
Cleary, Beverly, & Zelinsky, Paul O. (Illustrator). (2000). *Dear Mr. Henshaw.* Camelot. Addresses: Divorce and being new in town. For ages 9-12.
Cleary, Beverly, & Zelinsky, Paul O. (Illustrator). (1992). *Strider.* Avon. Addresses: Divorce and friendship. For ages 9-12.
Danziger, Paula, & Ross, Tony. (Illustrator). (1996). *Amber Brown wants extra credit.* Putnam. Addresses: Divorce. For ages 4-8.
Danziger, Paula, Ross, Tony (Illustrator), & Rogers, Jacqueline (Illustrator). (1998). *Amber Brown sees red.* Little Apple. Addresses: Divorce. For ages 9-12.
Fenner, Carol. (2000). *Randall's wall.* Aladdin. Addresses: Divorce. For ages 9-12.
Fenner, Carol. (2000). *The king of dragons.* Aladdin. Addresses: Poverty & homelessness. For ages 9-12.
Girard, Linda Walvoord, Friedman, Judith (Illustrator), & Levine, Abby (Editor). *At Daddy's on Saturdays.* Albert Whitman & Co. Addresses: Divorce. For ages 4-8.
Hahn, Mary Downing. (1998). *Following my own footsteps.* Camelot. Addresses: Abuse. For ages 9-12.
Hermes, Patricia. (1998). *Cheat the moon: A novel.* Little, Brown. Addresses: Parental neglect. For ages 9-12.
Lexau, Joan M., & Wilson, John (Illustrator). (1997). *Striped ice cream.* Scholastic. Addresses: Poverty. For ages 9-12.
Lowry, Lois, & Kelly, True. (Illustrator). (1997). *Stay: Keeper's story.* Houghton Mifflin. Addresses: Poverty. For ages 9-12.
Mario, Heidi Stetson. (Illustrator). (1998). *I'd rather have an iguana.* Charlesbridge. Addresses: New sibling. For ages 4-8.
Mayer, Mercer. (1985). *The new baby.* Golden Books. Addresses: New sibling. For ages 4-8.
McCourt, Lisa, & Ladwig, Tim (Illustrator). (1998). *Chicken soup for little souls: The braids girl.* Health Communications. Addresses: Poverty. For ages 4-8.
Napoli, Donna Jo. (2000). *Changing tunes.* Addresses: Divorce. For ages 9-12.
Park, Barbara. (1990). *Don't make me smile.* Random House Children's Publishers. Addresses: Divorce. For ages 9-12.
Peck, Richard. (2000). *Strays like us.* Puffin. Addresses: Poverty, parental drug abuse, being new in school. For ages 9-12.
Ryan, Pam Munoz. (2000). *Esperanza rising.* Scholastic. Addresses: Poverty and loss. For ages 9-12.
Siebold, Jan, & Shanahan, Denise. (2000). *Rope burn.* Albert Whitman & Co. Addresses: Divorce and being new in neighborhood. For ages 9-12.
Swan-Jackson, Alys, Klebanoff, Susan, Rosenfield, Lynn (contributor), & Shapiro, Joan (contributor). (1998). *When your parents split up: How to keep yourself together (plugged in).* Price Stern Sloan. Addresses: Divorce. For ages 9-12.
Winthrop, E., & Sandin, J. (Illustrator). (1998). *As the crow flies.* Clarion. Addresses: Divorce. For ages 4-8.

Chapter 3
Differing Cultures and the Morality of Schooling

Maria A. Pacino

One summer day, my 8-year-old daughter Vanessa, who had been playing with the neighborhood children, ran into the house crying. "Mommy, mommy, something is wrong. We were playing; they got mad at me and started yelling. They called me a n——. What does that mean? It must be something bad because all the kids ran away after saying it." My first reaction was shock. I really did not know what to say. Because Vanessa has a dark complexion (her background is Portuguese and Italian), made darker by the sun, she was the target of racial prejudice. My husband was angry and suggested that I call the parents of Vanessa's playmates to discuss the incident. Yet, I knew that the children had probably learned such attitudes in their homes. I tried to explain to my daughter that some people, out of ignorance, mistreat those who are different from them.

The following year, in 3rd grade, Vanessa brought home an essay she had written in class. My heart broke again when I read her words: "I wish I could change the color of my skin; I want to have lighter skin—like the other kids in my school." I thought about asking Vanessa's teacher to address issues of prejudice and cultural difference. Instead, I talked to Vanessa myself and reassured her that she did not have to be ashamed of her ethnic background or the color of her skin. I knew that she wanted to believe me, but she was receiving a different message at school.

When Vanessa reached middle school, another incident took place. One of the boys sitting in front of Vanessa turned around and said "You're as black as stone." (His knowledge of stones was apparently limited!) By now, Vanessa had learned to use language as a weapon in response to such comments. She replied, "I may be as black as stone, but I am much smarter than you because I would never be as mean as you to another person." I am sure the boy had not meant to be malicious. Nevertheless, teasing and bullying among children and young adults can become a dangerous habit, and even lead to fighting and other forms of violence, including murder (need we be reminded of school shootings across the United States?).

One morning after my girls (Vanessa, then 13, and Monique, a special education student, then 16) had already left for school, I went into our den and noticed writing all over the outside of the windows. Apparently during the night someone had vandalized our home, using racist language and symbols, many of which were unknown to us. My husband, my children, and I could not understand the reason for such a destructive, malicious act. The police examined the evidence and wrote out a report, but dismissed the actions as "just a bunch of kids playing around." Vanessa pointed out that people in the neighborhood did not seem to want us as neighbors. In my naiveté, I could not understand such prejudice and discrimination among neighbors who otherwise appeared to be friendly.

When Vanessa was in high school, she encountered prejudice from one of her English teachers. Each essay Vanessa wrote was marked heavily in red with demeaning comments, such as "poor writing." Vanessa began to lose confidence in her writing ability. In the class, her voice was silenced and her ideas dismissed. Consequently, her development suffered. She was humiliated further when the teacher told the other students that Vanessa was a poor writer—"the worst writer I had ever known!" Whenever the class was asked to do group work, many of the students refused to have Vanessa join their group. Meanwhile, I tried to make light of the situation. I told Vanessa that she needed to work harder and prove herself and that she should ignore the other kids. (I would handle the situation differently today!) Remembering the difficult times I had experienced as an adult immigrant, I wanted Vanessa to grow up strong and learn to stand up for herself. But Vanessa would say, "Mom, you don't understand—Mr. W. is prejudiced against me."

Looking back, I realized that I dismissed Vanessa's allegations because I was in denial. I wanted my child to fit in and succeed. I wanted her to develop the cognitive flexibility and the coping skills that would enable her to learn from life's stresses without being crushed by them. Fortunately, Vanessa managed to develop, essentially on her own, what Antonovsky (1987) calls "a sense of coherence," which allows individuals to select, metacognitively, the appropriate coping mechanism in a given stressful situation. Those with a strong sense of coherence are able to evaluate the situation and respond to stress according to its comprehensibility (it can be explained); manageability (it can be managed with appropriate resources); and meaningfulness (its validity as a learning experience).

Over the years, Vanessa, a bright and sensitive child, developed ways of coping with her school situation by using a measure of cynicism mixed with the power of words. Strong enough to avoid victimization, Vanessa developed her own sense of coherence through family and spiritual values. She is now a strong, self-assured young woman.

A Story Told Many Times

I found it difficult to explain racism to my daughter because the concept of race has no solid foundation or meaning in today's studies about culture. The old notions of race were used to support prejudice and discrimination. In social sciences, they have been replaced to a large degree by concepts of "ethnicity," which are more appropriate and useful. In *Man's Most Dangerous Myth: The Fallacy of Race*, Montagu (1997) defines race as a social construct that has no biological determination for one's mental ability, or physical grouping. He further states that "racism is wrong . . . [and] what is morally wrong cannot be politically right" (Montagu, 1997, p. 37). Racism, in part defined as holding a negative attitude toward culturally different individuals, is based on the belief that individual differences are determined by genetics. Regardless of the evidence, the general public still continues to use the term "race."

I wanted my daughter to be educated about cultural differences and similarities, and not confront these inequity issues merely from an emotional basis. I wanted her to understand that prejudice is an attitude that, if left "untreated" and ignored, may lead to a discriminatory pattern of behavior. I reminded her of the many incidences recorded in history of people being destroyed because of bigotry—ethnic cleansing, religious intolerance, and other social injustices (still being perpetrated today in the United States and abroad). I wanted Vanessa to consider the dangers of stereotyping, prejudice, and discrimination from within a historical context. I wanted her to understand that racist attitudes and behaviors are born of ignorance about and fear of those who are different. I hoped that her school curriculum and her teachers would present a balanced view of history that did more than just skim the surface of equity and social injustice. I hoped that her school experience would be academically and morally relevant to democratic citizenship.

Actually, I was having difficulty understanding the prejudice and discrimination we found in American schools. As a voluntary immigrant who had studied American history abroad, I thought that civil rights legislation had brought awareness and understanding to this democratic nation. Coming to the

United States was an eye-opening experience for me and I experienced several painful and humiliating moments. Watching my daughter facing prejudice and discrimination was painful for me at a time when I was negotiating my own acculturation process. Like any parent, however, I gladly would have taken on my child's pain as well, if I could.

Vanessa's experience with prejudice and discrimination extended beyond the school walls. We lived in a midwestern city that barely tolerated cultural differences (although the people were nice and helpful during winter storms!). The teachers and students in Vanessa's school were primarily white, middle-class, and Protestant, and displayed a limited perspective of world cultures. Vanessa, her sister, and two African American girls (who lived in our apartment complex) seemed to be the odd ones out. I remember going to a birthday party at our neighbor's home and sensing my African American neighbor's discomfort with the school situation. But I was naive, and we both felt powerless. The African American family moved out of the neighborhood the following year.

When we first moved to this midwestern city in 1974, I was watching the local news one morning on television. I could not believe what I was seeing—the Ku Klux Klan was marching through the streets of a nearby town! In fact, the KKK headquarters was located within 30 miles of this city. I learned that some of the students where I was teaching were children of KKK members. I felt fortunate that Mrs. Rowe, an African American teaching assistant at my school, became a good friend and surrogate mother to me. She helped me understand issues of ethnic prejudice and discrimination, offering her perspective and lessons learned from her experiences. She would drive me through her neighborhood, pointing to the dilapidated buildings and describing the poverty that leads to a sense of hopelessness. The implicit and explicit messages of social injustice I learned will remain forever in my memory. At the city schools where I taught, I often would hear demeaning remarks about children of color from fellow teachers and staff members—painful reminders that those who were different did not fit into their world. (I remember being told that I would not be able to attend a dinner at the local country club because of the color of my skin.)

Gregory Williams, who had lived in the same midwestern town, in Mrs. Rowe's neighborhood, reviews these painful issues in his book *Life on the Color Line* (1995). As a biracial student, he had been considered white until a teacher discovered his African American heritage. Thereafter, Gregory's life and treatment in that city changed. His white friends no longer accepted him. In fact, he was rejected by both whites and blacks! The story of how he struggled in a hostile and stressful school climate is remarkable. His apparent sense of coherence enabled him to cope, and eventually succeed in becoming the dean of a midwestern law school. Unfortunately, the ugly aspects of Williams's story are not unique. Neither is Vanessa's story. Stories of victimization by prejudice and discrimination are still being reported by ethnic minority children, especially those of immigrants who come to America "in pursuit of happiness."

The Stress of Acculturation

Acculturation can become stressful for some children, as they struggle with the complex task of managing their own cultural values and beliefs within a new culture with a different value and belief system. Furthermore, when differences are viewed as deficiencies rather than assets, children can be placed at risk. This is the case for many immigrant children, whose ethnicity, language, religion, values, norms, and behaviors tend to differ from those of the mainstream culture. Their marginality is worsened when the ethnic differences are openly displayed. Cultural traditions can be the source of conflict between parents and children, and among the school community. Immigrant children in California, for example, have felt the additional sting of referendums that carried an anti-immigrant sentiment. These laws make them feel insecure and unwelcome. Their self-image, their identity within the ethnic group, and their performance in school were inescapably affected. Although Vanessa was born in the United States and I was a legal resident, we both seemed to be questioning our ethnic identity, and even considering rejecting part of it for the sake of "fitting in."

Olsen's study (1997) of newly arrived immigrant students in a prototypical American public high school offers poignant insights on the stresses experienced by these adolescents. Some of her interviews reveal a sense of futility, embarrassment, and low self-worth. For example, a teenager who came from Afghanistan expressed the anxiety she felt and perceived in other immigrants: "most of us wish to be Americans. . . . We can speak English; we can wear the clothes. But we aren't the right religion; we aren't the same" (Olsen, 1997, p. 43). A Mexican immigrant student shared similar insights:

> Instead of [discriminating against] the immigrants, the native [born] should help them out so that we all together could heal the world. I think the teachers should . . . talk about racism, to teach their students not to discriminate [against] or segregate with other races. (Olsen, 1997, p. 50)

Another student, a Vietnamese immigrant, remarked on his struggle with conflicting values between cultures: "People ask me, why can't you be both Vietnamese and American? It just doesn't work because you run into too many contradictions" (Olsen, 1997, p. 54).

It is interesting to note that the white teenagers tended to deny that racism and discrimination existed in their school; they felt uncomfortable talking about race and social justice. They also expressed resentment toward affirmative action, which they considered to be reverse discrimination and special treatment given to people of color.

These young people's comments helped me validate Vanessa's story. It made me realize that schools can affect how children cope with cultural differences. Teachers' attitudes toward cultural differences affect their expectations and treatment of students. As one who teaches courses on diversity to teachers and administrators, I have witnessed some of my students' discomfort toward a large minority student population. These university students often feel uncomfortable engaging in critical inquiry regarding the impact of race, prejudice, and discrimination on schoolchildren. When confronted with issues of race, oppression, and social equity, some of the students tend to shift the discussion toward gender issues in order to diffuse conflict. Typical remarks from teachers and school administrators are:

> I'm tired for being blamed for whatever happened to Blacks and Native Americans in the past. . . . I'm angry about reverse discrimination. . . . I don't see the need for affirmative action anymore. They walk around with a chip on their shoulder; they are taking all the jobs, even if they are not qualified. I don't see color; I treat all my students the same. It is time to move on.

Unfortunately, these remarks are not uncommon in schools, even among higher education faculty. My role in teaching these courses is to ensure that teachers and administrators model respect for cultural diversity; provide nurturing classrooms to all children; and adopt anti-bias curriculum and equity pedagogy. Democratic classrooms rely on effective, meaningful relationships between teachers and students.

Although immigrant students try to interact with teachers and peers, and try to conform to the school culture, they are often unaware of larger sociocultural forces that shape their lives. Stressors in the lives of immigrant children include not only the academic, linguistic, and social challenges at school, but also issues of identity, self-esteem, and conflict between parental values and school values (Igoa, 1995; McLean Taylor, Gilligan, & Sullivan, 1995; Olsen, 1997). My husband, a first-generation Italian immigrant, recalls feeling embarrassed and out of place in a classroom where he was the only child who did not speak English. After learning the language, he then became the "culture broker" between his parents and the school.

Typically, schools consider immigrant students as problems rather than resources. Bilingual programs use primarily transitional methods (which focus on English only) rather than the recommended maintenance approach (which affirms the student's cultural identity and language, while adding a new culture and linguistic proficiency). School becomes an arena for negotiation in the daily lives of these children as they try to balance these newly acquired cultural habits with the older ones of their parents and extended family.

In *The Inner World of the Immigrant Child* (1995), Igoa describes the stresses of acculturation and their impact on immigrant children. The explicit and implicit messages sent by school policies and personnel, especially in literacy programs, can invalidate a child's sense of ethnic identity. Such struggles in school often lead to feelings of isolation, loneliness, and alienation. Many of these children will stay silent for extended periods in the classrooms. On other occasions, immigrant children's voices are silenced when teachers and other students reject the newcomers' mode of expression, language, and culture. One child, in expressing her loneliness, said: "I was lonely and alone and sad. I wasn't sure I could still make it in school. . . . I didn't know anyone and I didn't speak English" (Igoa, 1995, p. 91).

The conflict between the school's values and norms and those of the family can lead to so-called culture shock (an inability to function within the new culture). The resulting stress may necessitate counseling for immigrant children. Since children spend most of their day at school, it is important for educators to create classroom environments that affirm children's cultural identities.

Affirming a Child's Sense of Identity

Teachers often believe that children, especially very young children, are not aware of cultural or ethnic differences; research studies (e.g., Banks & Banks, 1997; Clark, 1955; Coles, 1964; Derman-Sparks & the ABC Task Force, 1989; Goodman, 1952; Ramsey, 1987), however, have found that children's racial attitudes mirror those of adults, and that children not only notice but also are inquisitive about ethnic differences. When children of color seem to identify, for example, with Eurocentric, mainstream ethnic preferences, they may not necessarily be rejecting their identity, but rather seeking to fit in within the school's social structure.

Research studies by Goodman (1952), Clark (1955), Coles (1964), among others, indicate that children as young as 2 are aware of differences in ethnicity, language, and gender. Children ages 3 to 5 are interested in the physical characteristics of others and themselves. From 5 to 9 years old, children show interest in, and better understand, cultural differences of race and national identity, and they begin to feel pride in their own cultures. Starting at ages 9 to 12, children can understand ethnic and ancestral identity differences.

Clark's (1955) studies with dolls and black children indicated that the black children preferred white dolls 75 percent of the time. Clark also found that even non-African American children who were viewed as "dark" by mainstream society would accept society's racial definition of themselves, although it differed from the children's understanding of their own identity. Kenneth Clark, who believed that schooling contributed to children's personal, moral, and social stability, remarked on the contradictory messages of schools and other societal institutions:

> The same institutions that teach children the democratic and religious doctrines of brotherhood and the equality of all human beings—institutions such as the church and the school—also teach them to violate these concepts through racial prejudice and undemocratic behavior toward others . . . teachers and administrators [must] recognize their responsibilities in the area of racial practices and procedures. (Clark, 1955, pp. 78, 94)

Goodman's (1952) study with white children revealed that even 4-year-olds showed definite signs of racial bigotry. Goodman advocated using literature and storytelling as means for eradicating prejudice and discrimination in schools.

I was intrigued by McLean Taylor, Gilligan, and Sullivan's (1995) study regarding the acculturation process as experienced by a group of Portuguese girls, since that is my cultural background. These authors highlighted Christina, a Portuguese American immigrant. Christina would decide whether or not it was "safe" to speak out against any discrimination she faced depending on the situation at hand. DuBois (1909) defined this action as "double consciousness," or the ability to look at oneself through the eyes of others. Similar personal stories have been reported in studies by Galarza (1971), Rodriguez (1983), and Ponce (1993). These autobiographical accounts reveal the authors' angst in their acculturation process, the conflict between family values and school values, and the need to fit in while trying to maintain one's sense of cultural identity.

In her book *White Teacher*, Paley (2000) shares an early teaching experience at a school where one third of the children were students of color and the faculty was all white. Paley recalls an incident in a kindergarten classroom during which the children selected from among a variety of dolls:

> All the white children pointed to the white babies. Half of the black children pointed to the white babies, and half to the black babies. The Asian and Middle Eastern children vacillated between all types.... I had been caught up in white-black differences and Jewish-gentile differences. (Paley, 2000, p. 32)

Faced with the challenge of cultural diversity, the faculty at the school decided to adopt a color-blind perspective. Paley attempted to downplay things when children pointed out color differences. When teachers believe that they do not see color, however, they are risking devaluation of the identity of many children in their classrooms.

Paley recalls a white kindergarten child describing her African American classmate's color as resembling chocolate pudding. At that moment, Paley said she felt uncomfortable about the school's color-blind policy, as well as her own upbringing of showing respect by ignoring color. Faced with a moral imperative, she decided that it was time to move toward a curriculum that valued differences. She began talking openly with her young students about valuing and respecting the differences found in a pluralistic society.

Through sociological studies on acculturation and identity, researchers have developed adaptation typologies. Robert Merton (1957) developed a typology of individual adaptation with the following categories:

- Conformity (individuals accept the status quo—the most common mode in a stable society)
- Innovation (individuals adapt within a goal- and success-oriented society that encourages risk-taking)
- Ritualism (individuals reject the status quo, but engage in safe routines as an adaptation/coping mechanism for staying out of trouble)
- Retreatism (individuals reject the status quo and tend to isolate themselves from the larger society because they feel victimized—a process that may encourage the collective adaptation of marginalized individuals)
- Rebellion (individuals or groups rebel against the status quo and create their own social values and norms).

Merton's typology assumes that individual adaptation is affected by sociocultural influences.

Milton Bennet's (1986) adaptation typology, "Levels of Intercultural Sensitivity," includes three Ethnocentric stages, followed by three Ethnorelative stages. The Ethnocentric stages are:

- Denial of Difference (individuals deny the existence of cultural differences, because they lack exposure to cultural diversity, or they opt for isolation or separation from other cultures)
- Defense Against Difference (individuals view cultural differences as deficits, blame the victim for lack of opportunity, and resent affirmative action; at this stage, Reversal may occur, as some minorities denigrate their own culture and view the dominant culture as superior)
- Minimization of Difference (individuals tend to approach cultural differences as superficial and "exotic"; they use their "cultural lenses" to evaluate other cultures and espouse the "melting pot" paradigm and acculturation through assimilation; they believe in the myth of a colorblind society).

The Ethnorelative states are:

- Acceptance of Difference (individuals recognize and accept cultural differences as assets)
- Adapting to Difference (individuals develop skills for effective communication across cultures)
- Integration of Differences (individuals internalize multicultural frames of reference, adopt a global perspective, view adaptation as cultural pluralism).

Educators should strive to move children from ethnocentrism to ethnorelativism, thereby reducing insensitivity toward cultural differences as well as reducing acculturation stress.

Banks (1995) examined the issue of ethnic identity and identification and its impact on school children, pedagogy, and curriculum. He developed a typology of ethnic identity to help individuals identify their own stages of ethnicity and determine where other individuals are within those stages. The goal is to move toward acceptance and praise of cultural differences in oneself and others. Banks reminds us that this typology is complex and nonlinear; moving within the stages is a gradual, developmental process, which is affected by the individual's experiences in society. For example, a person whose ethnic identity is threatened or rejected may revert to an ethnocentric attitude. This type of experience leads to high stress levels, especially in children. A democratic society must allow individuals to feel secure within their ethnic identities if they are to participate in and contribute to the society as a whole.

One's sense of self is deeply rooted in a healthy notion of ethnic and cultural identity. When teachers examine their own ethnic identities and historical roots, they are better able to help children affirm their ethnic identities and to ease them through the acculturation process, thereby reducing stress. When children of different cultural backgrounds are socialized within a mainstream society, they tend to adopt bicultural attitudes as a means of fitting into both worlds—mainstream society and their own ethnic group. Although Delpit (1994) believes in affirming children's ethnic identity, she also feels that culturally different children must learn to negotiate mainstream society so that they can function effectively within it. Delpit states that if the system is not going to accommodate minorities, then they need to make adjustments. Mainstream society also needs to make accommodations, in part by having classrooms assume the responsibility for acculturation.

Creating Caring Classrooms Through Multicultural Education

Through multicultural education, students learn to address issues of social justice and actively engage in combating racism, prejudice, and discrimination. Multicultural education affirms ethnic identities; provides solutions to intercultural conflicts; and, through curricular interventions, helps reduce prejudice and manage children's stress. Teaching children to regard cultural differences as assets helps eradicate misconceptions about ethnicity, language, gender, religion, socioeconomic status, and disability (Banks, 1995; Derman Sparks & the ABC Task Force, 1989; Ramsey, 1987).

Studies reveal that reducing prejudice can be achieved if certain conditions remain constant. Teachers and schools need to create democratic classrooms in which culturally different students feel that they are part of a community by "knowing each other as individuals; having equal status and sharing common interests, as well as [developing] a favorable climate established by an authority figure" (Smardo & Schmidt, 1983, p. 25)

Classroom activities and discussions can help children develop healthy and positive attitudes about race and other cultural differences. By reading and discussing meaningful multicultural literature, including autobiographies, students learn to recognize stereotypes and develop more positive outlooks. Children need access to quality multicultural materials that provide accurate ethnic information. Anti-bias, equity-based, multicultural curriculum and instructional materials (literature, videos, toys, simulations, service/learning) allow educators and parents to teach children respect and appreciation for cultural differences; caring and responsibility in a global community; and ethical/moral, reflective decision-making.

Through multicultural education, students gain the skills to function across cultures without rejecting their own ethnic identities. They become proud of their heritage and learn to perceive and understand multiple cultural interpretations of values, beliefs, and behaviors, while eliminating ethnocentric views, stereotypes, and racist attitudes. An anti-bias curriculum creates school environments that nurture children, affirm their diversity, and help them resolve conflicts in creative, rather than destructive, ways. Schools and teachers must shift acculturation paradigms away from the melting pot perspective toward cultural pluralism, they must apply these principles to curriculum design and pedagogy, and they must use transformation and social action approaches in critical inquiry and problem solving. When students examine issues from multiple viewpoints, they learn to accept and respect cultural differences and become responsive to sociocultural challenges.

Literature—including personal narratives and storytelling—can be a tool that allows individuals to examine their cultural roots, belief systems, and connections to society. For immigrant children and children of color, multicultural literature can be liberating as it facilitates acculturation and connection to a new community, while promoting pride in their ethnic heritages. Multicultural books also serve as cultural and linguistic mirrors that affirm differences, allow readers to examine issues of social justice from other points of view, and provide connections to the community. When students and teachers collaborate and share their voices in reading and writing, they begin to define and discover their sense of self.

When using multicultural literature, educators must consider literary merit, values-centered themes, and cultural authenticity. Educators should use appropriate anti-biased, inclusive criteria that affirm cultural and linguistic differences while providing authentic, balanced portrayals of relationships across cultures, even when conflicts are present. Characters in multicultural literature should be portrayed realistically and with dignity; books should be available that show minority characters in positions of power, as inspiration for the children. See Lindgren (1990) for additional criteria to use when selecting multicultural materials.

It is probably unrealistic to expect educators to be knowledgeable about all cultural backgrounds; however, educators can learn a great deal from the students themselves, their parents, and the community. Teachers need to make the effort to get to know their students and understand their varied experiences and cultural backgrounds. Educators must model the ethic of caring with students, parents, and community.

The Moral Undertaking of Teaching and Learning

Children's development of moral reasoning occurs in stages (Coles, 1997; Kohlberg, 1981; Piaget, 1965). These moral development stages—from early childhood on—can be nurtured through equity pedagogy and anti-bias curriculum. Teaching caring, respect, and cultural awareness through literature encourages learners to focus on the ethical dimension of a story, and to analyze historical events from multiple perspectives. A discussion based on social transformation will aid students in making ethical choices in their lives. Character education programs, conducted in conjunction with parents and with community organizations, give teachers opportunities to engage students in discussions that foster moral interaction and ethical reflection. Character education is often integrated through a multicultural literature curriculum and reinforced with community service/learning activities.

Many schools also require students to perform community service as a means of developing a commitment to social action. Character education programs often include conflict resolution strategies/skills training to facilitate intercultural communication, understanding, and respect. One program, Peace Patrol, uses peers to mediate conflict. School principals report that using the program reduced incidents of racial conflict on their campuses, and increased cultural awareness and respect for cultural differences.

When ethical issues are woven through the curriculum through cooperative learning and grouping, students learn to listen and to mediate conflict in ways that respect diversity and the democratic process. A caring community helps create such a school culture, in which teachers take the role of responsive mentors who model and guide learners in developing critical consciousness and moral reflection (Coles, 1997; Jackson, Boostrom, & Hansen, 1998; Noddings, 1984). Such moral, caring classrooms reduce stress levels among culturally different children. As moral education is an important part of schooling for a diverse society, schools should be designed to support and nurture the ethic of caring.

The following quote illustrates the responsibility of educators for creating caring, culturally responsive, and morally responsive classrooms:

> Teachers are human beings who bring their cultural perspectives, values, hopes, and dreams to the classroom. They also bring their prejudices, stereotypes, and misconceptions to the classroom. . . . It is important for them to come to grips with their own personal cultural values and identities in order for them to help students from diverse racial, ethnic, and cultural groups to develop clarified cultural identities and to relate positively to each other. (Sleeter, 1991, p. 139)

Schools and educators must question whether or not their policies and practices model ethical attitudes and behaviors. For example, a teacher who asks the class to collect canned foods at Thanksgiving but does not talk about issues of hunger, homelessness, and social justice sends an ambiguous message to the students.

Teachers and administrators need to be aware of the moral consequences of schooling. A teacher who overhears racial slurs and does nothing about it, or is uncomfortable confronting the issue, is compromising the moral integrity of the community of learners. Words can hurt; for some children, frequently hearing the word "black" associated with a negative connotation (such as in the phrase "the black sheep of the family") can have a negative effect on their levels of self-esteem, thus increasing their stress levels. Teachers who sanitize curriculum to avoid dealing with issues of oppression and injustice, within historical contexts, fail to model critical inquiry and moral responsibility.

Schools must foster: intellectual discourse among a community of learners committed to a transformative, social action, equity-based curriculum; spiritual development within diversity; and responsible, participatory citizenship. Schools are an essential element in efforts to develop the moral consciousness of a nation in a pluralistic democracy. The following pledge taken by children at the World of Difference Institute could serve as a moral anchor for schools and other societal institutions:

> I pledge from this day onward to do my best to interrupt prejudice and to stop those who, because of hate, would hurt, harass, or violate the civil rights of anyone. I will try at all times to be aware of my own biases against people who are different from myself. . . . I will speak out against anyone who mocks, seeks to intimidate, or actually hurts someone of a different race, religion, ethnic group, or sexual orientation. . . . I will think about specific ways my school, other students, and my community can promote respect for people and create a prejudice-free zone. I firmly believe that one person can make a difference. (Stern-LaRosa & Hofheimer Bettmann, 2000, p. 280)

My own personal experience and insights as an immigrant, a mother, and an educator reveal that the teaching and learning process requires reciprocal relationships within the community of learners. I have a responsibility to make my students understand the physical and emotional pain associated with prejudice and discrimination. My students, as teachers and administrators, need to recognize how culturally insensitive remarks and behavior can bring on stress. They must make sure that their schools and classrooms will not tolerate demeaning and demoralizing attitudes toward culturally different children. When I stand in the classroom with my students, I need to be authentic, morally accountable, and even, at times, vulnerable; I must remind myself that education is a spiritual journey, and that "teaching holds a mirror to the soul" (Palmer, 1995, p. 15).

References

Antonovsky, Aaron. (1987). *Unraveling the mystery of health: How people manage stress and stay well.* San Francisco: Jossey-Bass.

Banks, James. (1995). *Teaching strategies for ethnic studies.* Boston: Allyn and Bacon.

Banks, James, & Banks, Cherry. (1997). *Multicultural education: Issues and perspectives.* Boston: Allyn & Bacon.

Bennett, Milton J. (1986). A developmental approach to training intercultural sensitivity. *International Journal of Intercultural Relations, 10*(2), 179-96.

Clark, Kenneth B. (1955). *Prejudice and your child.* Boston: Beacon Press.

Coles, Robert. (1964). *Children of crisis: A study of courage and fear.* Boston: Little, Brown.

Coles, Robert. (1997). *The moral intelligence of children.* New York: Random House.

Delpit, Lisa. (1994). Seeing color: A review of *White Teacher.* In *Rethinking our schools: Teaching for equity and justice* (pp. 130-132). Milwaukee, WI: Rethinking Schools.

Derman-Sparks, Louise, & the ABC Task Force. (1989). *Anti-bias curriculum: Tools for empowering young children.* Washington, DC: National Association for the Education of Young Children.

Dubois, W. E. B. (1909). *The souls of black folk.* Chicago, IL: A.C. McClurg.

Galarza, Ernesto. (1971). *Barrio boy.* South Bend, IN: University of Notre Dame Press.

Goodman, Mary Ellen. (1952). *Race awareness in young children.* Cambridge, MA: Addison-Wesley.

Igoa, Cristina. (1995). *The inner world of the immigrant child.* New York: St. Martin Press.

Jackson, Philip W., Boostrom, Robert E., & Hansen, David T. (1998). *The moral life of schools.* San Francisco: Jossey-Bass.

Kohlberg, Lawrence. (1981). *The philosophy of moral development: Moral stages and the idea of justice: Essays on moral development, 1.* San Francisco: Harper and Row.

Lindgren, Merri V. (Ed.). (1990). *The multicolored mirror.* Fort Atkinson, WI: Highsmith.

McLean Taylor, Jill, Gilligan, Carol, & Sullivan, Amy. (1995). *Between voice and silence: Women and girls: Race and relationship.* Cambridge, MA: Harvard University Press.

Merton, Robert K. (1957). *Social theory and social structure.* New York: Free Press.

Montagu, Ashley. (1997). *Man's most dangerous myth: The fallacy of race* (6th ed.). Walnut Creek, CA: Altamira Press.

Noddings, Nel. (1984). *Caring: A feminine approach to ethics & moral education.* Berkeley, CA: University of California Press.

Olsen, Laurie. (1997). *Made in America: Immigrant students in our public schools.* New York: The New Press.

Paley, Vivian Gussin. (2000). *White teacher.* Cambridge, MA: Harvard University Press.

Palmer, Parker J. (1997). The heart of a teacher: Identity and integrity in teaching. *Change, 29*(6), 15-21.

Piaget, Jean. (1965). *The moral judgment of the child.* New York: Free Press.
Ponce, Mary Helen. (1993). *Hoyt Street: An autobiography.* Albuquerque, NM: University of New Mexico Press.
Ramsey, Patricia G. (1987). *Teaching and learning in a diverse world.* New York: Teachers College Press.
Rodriguez, Richard. (1983). *Hunger of memory.* New York: Bantam.
Sleeter, Christine E. (1991). *Empowerment through multicultural education.* Albany, NY: State University of New York.
Smardo, Frances A., & Schmidt, Velma. (1983). Developing multicultural awareness. *Children Today, 12*(May-June), 23-25.
Stern-LaRosa, Caryl, & Hofheimer Bettmann, Ellen. (2000). *The Anti-Defamation League's Hate hurts: How children learn and unlearn prejudice.* New York: Scholastic.
Williams, Gregory H. (1995). *Life on the color line.* New York: Penguin

Recommended Multicultural Books for Children

Adler, David. (1987). *The number on my grandfather's arm.* New York: Union of American Hebrew Congregational Press.
Adoff, Arnold. (1982). *All the colors of the race.* New York: Lothrop, Lee & Shepard.
Anaya, Rudolfo A. (1976). *Heart of Aztlan.* Albuquerque, NM: University of New Mexico Press.
Armstrong, Jennifer. (1992). *Steal away . . . to freedom.* New York: Scholastic.
Brimmer, Larry D. (1996). *A migrant family.* Minneapolis, MN: Lerner Publishing.
Bunting, Eve. (1990). *The wall.* New York: Clarion.
Bunting, Eve. (1994). *Smoky night.* New York: Clarion.
Burns Knight, Margy. (1993). *Who belongs here? An American story.* Gardiner, ME: Tilbury House.
Clifton, Lucille. (1973). *All of us come across the water.* Austin, TX: Holt, Rinehart and Winston.
Coerr, Eleanor. (1977). *Sadako and a thousand cranes.* New York: Dell.
Cohen, Barbara. (1983). *Molly's pilgrim.* New York: Lothrop, Lee, & Shepard.
Coles, Robert. (1995). *The story of Ruby Bridges.* New York: Scholastic.
Dorros, Arthur. (1991). *Abuela.* New York: E. P. Dutton.
Hamanaka, Sheila. (1990). *The journey: Japanese Americans, racism and renewal.* New York: Orchard Books.
Hamilton, Virginia. (1988). *Anthony Burns: The defeat and triumph of a fugitive slave.* New York: Knopf.
Hewett, Joan. (1990). *Hector lives in the United States now.* Philadelphia, PA: J. B. Lippincott.
Hoffman, Mary. (1991). *Amazing Grace.* New York: Dial Books.
Houston, Jeanne W., & Houston, James D. (1983). *Farewell to Manzanar.* New York: Bantam.
Hoyt-Goldsmith, Diane. (1991). *Pueblo storyteller.* New York: Holiday House.
Jenness, Aylette. (1990). *Families: A celebration of diversity, commitment and love.* New York: Houghton Mifflin.
Kogoa, Joy N. (1986). *Naomi's road.* New York: Oxford University Press.
Lomas Garza, C. (1990). *Family pictures/Cuadros de familia.* San Francisco: Children's Book Press.
Lord, Betty B. (1984). *In the year of the boar and Jackie Robinson.* New York: Harper.
Mohr, Nicholasa. (1989). *Felita.* New York: Bantam.
Paek, Min. (1978). *Aekyungs's dream.* San Francisco: Children's Book Press.
Soto, Gary. (1990). *Baseball in April and other stories.* New York: Harcourt Brace Jovanovich.
Yep, Laurence. (1993). *Dragon's gate.* New York: HarperCollins.

Other Resources for Teachers

Vidcos
A class divided. (PBS) 1-800-344-3337
American cultures for children. (Library Video Company)
Different and the same: Helping children identify and prevent prejudice. (Family Communications, Inc.)

Web Sites
Anti-Defamation League: www.adl.org
Multicultural Book Review: www.isomedia.com/homes/jmele/homepage
Multicultural Pavilion: http://curry.edschool.Virginia.EDU/go/multicultural
Multicultural Publishing and Educational Council: www.mpec.org
Museum of Toleranc: www.wiesenthal.com
National Multicultural Institute: www.nmci.org
National Network of Family Resiliency: www.schoolnet.co/home/e/

Bibliography

Allen, Andrew. (1997). Creating space for discussions about social justice and equity in an elementary classroom. *Language Arts, 24*(7), 518-24.

Banks, James, & Banks, Cherry. (1997). *Multicultural education: Issues and perspectives.* Boston: Allyn & Bacon.

Baruth, Leroy G., & Manning, M. L. (1992). *Multicultural education of children and adolescents.* Boston: Allyn and Bacon.

Betz-Zall, Jonathan. (1995). Balancing quality and relevance: Selecting series biographies for children about women and people of color. *Multicultural Review, 2*(3), 34-42.

Byrnes, Deborah A., & Kiger, Gary. (Eds.). (1997). *Common bonds: Anti-bias teaching in a diverse society* (2nd ed.). Olney, MD: Association for Childhood Education International.

Cahill, Susan. (1995). *Growing up female: Stories by women writers from the American mosaic.* New York: Mentor.

Campbell, Laura A. (1999). *Storybooks for tough times.* Golden, CO: Fulcrum Resources.

Carson, David K., & Swanson, Dee M. (1992). Stress and coping as predicators of young children's development and psychological adjustment. *Child Study Journal, 24*(4), 273-297.

Chavez, David, Moran, Virginia P., Reid, Suzanne L., & Lopez, Muriel. (1997). Acculturation stress in children. *Hispanic Journal of Behavioral Sciences, 19,* 34-35.

Day, Frances A. (1994). *Multicultural voices in contemporary literature.* Portsmouth, NH: Heinemann.

Delpit, Lisa. (1995). *Other people's children.* New York: The New Press.

De Melendez, Wilma R., & Ostertag, Vesna. (1997). *Teaching young children in multicultural classrooms.* New York: Delmar Publishers.

Diamond, Barbara J., & Moore, Margaret A. (1995). *Multicultural literacy.* Reston, VA: Longman.

Esquivel, Gisele B., & Keitel, Merle A. (1990). Counseling immigrant children. *Elementary School Guidance & Counseling, 24,* 213-219.

Fraser, Steven. (1995). *The bell curve wars: Race, intelligence, and the future of America.* New York: Basic Books.

Frosh, Mary. (1994). *Coming of age in America.* New York: The New Press.

Garcia, Eugene. (1994). *Understanding and meeting the challenge of student cultural diversity.* Boston: Houghton Mifflin.

Glazer, Nathan. (1997). *We are all multiculturalists now.* Cambridge, MA: Harvard University Press.

Godina, Heriberto. (1996). The canonical debate: Implementing multicultural literature and perspectives. *Journal of Adolescent & Adult Literacy, 39*(7), 544-549.

Greer, Colin, & Kohl, Herbert. (1995). *A call to character: A family treasury of stories, poems, plays, proverbs, and fables to guide the development of values for you and your children.* New York: HarperCollins.

Hansen-Krening, Nancy, & Mizokawa, Donald T. (1997). Exploring ethnic-specific literature. *Journal of Adolescent & Adult Literacy, 41*(3), 180-188.

Hutner, Gordon. (1999). *Immigrant voices.* New York: Penguin Books.

Lantieri, Linda, & Patti, Janet. (1996). *Waging peace in our schools.* Boston: Beacon Press.

McCarthy, Cameron, & Crichlow, Warren. (1993). *Race identity and representation in education.* New York: Routledge.

Martin, Renee J. (1995). *Practicing what we teach.* Albany, NY: State University of New York Press.

Miller-Lachman, Lyn. (1992). *Our family, our friends, our world.* New York: R. R. Bowker.

Paley, Vivian Gussin. (1992). *You can't say you can't play.* Cambridge, MA: Harvard University Press.

Portes, Alejandro, & Rumbaut, Ruben G. (1996). *Immigrant America: A portrait.* Berkeley, CA: University of California Press.

Quintero, Elizabeth P., & Rummel, Mary K. (1998). *American voices: Webs of diversity.* Columbus, OH: Merrill.

Rasinski, Timothy V., & Padak, Nancy D. (1990). Multicultural learning through children's literature. *Language Arts, 67,* 576-80.

Rodriguez, Fred. (1999). *Affirming equity.* Dubuque, IA: Kendall/Hunt.

Ru, Victoria R., & Stremmel, Andrew J. (1999). *Affirming diversity through democratic conversations.* Columbus, OH: Merrill.

Schwartz, Elaine G. (1995). Crossing borders/shifting paradigms: Multiculturalism and children's literature. *Harvard Educational Review, 65*(4), 634-650.

Slapin, Beverly, & Seale, Doris. (1991). *Through Indian eyes.* Philadelphia, PA: New Society Publishers.

Swiniarski, Louise A., Breitborde, Mary-Lou, & Murphy, Jo-Anne. (1999). *Educating the global village.* Columbus, OH: Merrill.

Takaki, Ronald. (1993). *A different mirror: A history of multicultural America.* New York: Little, Brown.

Tiedt, Pamela L., & Tiedt, Iris M. (1995). *Multicultural teaching: A handbook of activities, information, and resources.* Boston: Allyn and Bacon.

Walker-Dalhouse, Doris. (1992). Using African-American literature to increase ethnic understanding. *The Reading Teacher, 45*(6), 416-422.

West, Cornell. (1994). *Race matters.* New York: Vintage Books.

Wheeler, Thomas C. (1971). *The immigrant experience: The anguish of becoming American.* New York: Penguin Books.

Wilkinson, Phyllis A., & Kido, Elissa. (1997). Literature and cultural awareness: Voices from the journey. *Language Arts, 74,* 255-265.

Chapter 4
Stress and Children With Disabilities

David P. Colachico

Robert is a child who has a hard time finding things in his room, and is regularly forgetting things—whether or not he fed the dog, where he left his textbook, what time he needs to leave for school. Each morning of the seven years that Robert has been attending school, he and his family follow the same routine. Nevertheless, Robert cannot seem to remember what to do, and each morning is chaotic. Many mornings end with Robert and his mother or father lecturing him about his lack of organization or the need to be ready to leave for school on time. Too often, Robert must rush out the door to meet the school bus. At school, Robert's teachers complain about his daydreaming and forgetfulness. Robert seems to have trouble paying attention. He often comes to class without his books or homework. Often, Robert cannot follow the lecture; instead, he daydreams about what he will do after school. He has trouble focusing his thoughts on the lesson or the homework assignment. His teachers frequently reprimand Robert for not sitting still and for being off-task. The regular calls home about Robert's behavior frustrate his parents, and they wonder what Robert's difficulties might be and how to overcome them.

Angela, a young girl who must use a wheelchair, does not keep her room in order. Her parents regularly ask her to clean her room, but the job never seems to get finished. Although her parents have helped Angela clean her room and demonstrated what to do, she does not seem to remember the process or feel capable of carrying it out. Angela tends to break a lot of things, and even injures herself. At school, the teachers find that Angela is either inattentive or she acts out. She pushes her classmates while waiting in line in the cafeteria, and she is overly demanding for attention on the playground. She has trouble remembering the routine set for her by her teacher, and often appears defiant. Angela uses her physical disability as an excuse for not performing a task in school. Angela's teacher and parents are frustrated by the situation. The resulting stress in the household leads to frequent arguments between Angela and her parents, or between her parents themselves.

Fred, month after month and year after year, has heard negative comments about himself from the people closest to him: "You're bad." "You're dumb." "You just don't understand." These comments eroded Fred's self-esteem to a point where he could not make decisions without feeling highly stressed. Fred became convinced that he was, indeed, stupid. He could not understand what was being presented in class. While he was able to follow what was being said in class, he could not write papers or get organized on his own. Fred's teachers and his parents frequently lectured him, and asked why he was not trying. Fred began to think that he was helpless to change the situation, and that it was easier to give up.

Types of Stress for the Child With Disabilities

The above individuals are not unique. Many children—especially those with disabilities—face similar experiences and feelings. Every young child has worries and feels stress to some degree. The term stress is used to describe the anxiety, conflict, frustration, emotional disturbance, and strain of survival.

It also describes any event to which a person must adapt or react (Cable, 1994).

The pressures felt by Robert, Angela, and Fred come from both outside (e.g., their teachers or parents) and from within (their own emotional responses). Often, a discrepancy exists between what a child is capable of doing and what others think he ought to be able to do.

Stress, a normal part of life, is unavoidable. It affects everyone, and children with disabilities face more than the average. Furthermore, they may not be able to understand the stressors or their reactions to them. Kirk and Gallagher (1989) classified four categories of stressors affecting children with disabilities:

- Child-related. Depending on such factors as the nature and severity of the disability and the child's age, the disabled child may have trouble handling his or her emotional reactions to the condition. Children with disabilities also experience a great deal of stress related to their own behavior and social responsiveness. With age, the stress may increase as the child prepares to leave school and enter the work force.
- Parent-generated. Parents may have unrealistic views of their child's ability and the goals that can be achieved. Thus, they place the child in a difficult position. Furthermore, this situation can lead to strained relationships between the two parents and, as the perceived cause of the stress, the child may feel the fall-out.
- Family structure and resource. The socioeconomic status of the family and the number of children in the family play a role in how a disability affects family stress levels. Having to purchase adaptive equipment or modify the home to meet the needs of a disabled child can tax a family's budget. In addition, siblings may resent the added attention that the child with disabilities receives.
- Social dynamics. A family may feel stigmatized or even embarrassed because their child has a disability. Parents also may have difficulty acknowledging the possibility that their child will not be able to support himself as an adult.

The Effects of Stress on Health

Stress can bring on numerous negative physical reactions in anybody. Children with disabilities are particularly subject to these problems. Furthermore, it becomes a vicious cycle as illness, poor nutrition, and sleep disorders are not uncommon among children with disabilities, as are headaches, stomach irritations, or even panic attacks. These physical symptoms produce more stress and anxiety.

Margalit and Ankonina (1991) found that children with disabilities, as well as their family members, could reduce the frequency or severity of health problems associated with stress by relying on a full repertoire of coping skills. A method that helps an individual to cope with one stressful situation may not work in another situation. Children with disabilities and their families need a variety of techniques to reduce anxiety and stress.

Severe or prolonged stress can bring about health problems (Large, 1999). Stress can, for example, worsen the symptoms of asthma, bronchitis, or other respiratory conditions. Stress can lessen the natural production of insulin, and lead over time to an onset of diabetes. Stress can inhibit the immune system and suppress the body's ability to repair tissue. Therefore, a stressed individual is more susceptible to colds and flu or other contagious illnesses (Cable, 1994). Children with chronic illnesses particularly need to learn to keep stress at a minimum.

Coping skills, by decreasing anxiety-related distractions, can also be helpful for children with behavior disorders, who may need help staying on task while doing school work. Many children with learning or behavior disorders must also contend with such stressors as poverty, child abuse, and neglect, which leaves them vulnerable to juvenile delinquency and gang membership (Jackson & Owens,

1999). Many of these children behave inappropriately as a defense mechanism against fear and distress, and so they may be isolated from a peer support system. The education experiences of many disabled children are poor, because they have trouble concentrating. All these factors jeopardize these children's ability to cope with stress, while actually adding to the stress they already are experiencing.

Helping children manage their stress levels will raise self-esteem and give children the feeling that they have gained control over their own negative behaviors. Such success may begin a chain of reinforcement, whereby the student is more likely to repeat the positive behavior. These outcomes are particularly beneficial when the child has a disability. Relaxation and movement exercises also decrease stress levels, improving body image and health (Jackson & Owens, 1999).

Public Law 94-142 (known as the Individual with Disabilities Education Act or IDEA) mandates that each disabled child must have a specific remediation plan, or Individualized Education Plan (IEP), designed by a team of professionals and the parents. Stress management strategies could be an important element of the IEP. A functional curriculum could include many of the strategies already listed. It also could involve the parents in the process of planning a stress-free environment for the child, both in school and at home. Each family's individual circumstances need to be considered, so that those who are involved with helping the child will better understand his or her particular stressors.

Understanding Families in Stress

Parents of children with disabilities have increased responsibilities beyond the regular, day-to-day ones necessary to keep a job and maintain a home. The disabled child often needs more attention than do nondisabled children, and painstaking training may be necessary to build and reinforce the skills required to manage the disability. What was quickly learned by a sibling may take weeks or months for the disabled child to learn. This process takes considerable effort and patience from family members. Health care, a constant concern, is also a matter of extra effort. Parents may have to be more vigilant, for example, in supervising the child's diet, even after the child has begun to mature. This can be very frustrating for a parent, especially when siblings have become much more independent.

According to Kaplan (1996), 28 percent of the parents raising children with chronic illnesses as a manifestation of a disability indicated that the disability was a stressor affecting the family's daily life. Sixty percent of the parents of children with multiple disabilities mentioned stress as having a primary impact on the family. Thus, a child's disability inevitably brings change to the family's dynamics. It was not surprising to discover that some studies (e.g., Kaplan, 1996) revealed that mothers of children with disabilities had higher incidents of depression and health problems, and they more often felt isolated.

Making accommodations for the needs of the disabled child (e.g., assistive devices, medications, modifications for wheelchair access) can become a financial strain for the family. In addition, one or both of the parents may need to leave work frequently to attend to their child, causing difficulties with employers.

The birth of a child with a disability causes exceptional stress. Often, parents feel guilty wondering if the child's disability is their fault. They wonder if something that they did could have caused the disability. The family is faced with many questions and few answers, and they may have to adjust their expectations for the child's future. At first, many parents go through a grieving process after they find out that their child has a disability. Common reactions include shock, denial, guilt, anger, and sadness. In the end, parents often learn to accept the situation. As soon as the child is identified with a disability, the family needs to locate public or private education intervention services. Early intervention is crucial, and so families must learn to cope as quickly as possible in order to acquire such services. As the child prepares to enter school, training should be centered on teaching the skills necessary for the child to understand instruction.

Parents may be of two minds about their child going to school; they want him to be able to do some of the same things as his peers, but not knowing what is happening in the child's day-to-day life when he is attending school may increase a parent's stress level. The child may sense the parent's unease and react in kind. The teacher, in turn, may have to contend with a child who has not been properly prepared to make his own decisions or maintain a schedule. She may feel stressed when daily needs are not being met or when deadlines are ignored.

Siblings of a disabled child may end up assuming more responsibility than other children their age—being a caretaker, performing chores that the disabled child cannot do—which may lead to resentment. They may even feel embarrassment about the disabled sibling's behavior (National Information Center for Children and Youth With Disabilities, 1988). Their increased stress levels will affect the rest of the family. Consequently, nondisabled siblings need as much special understanding, attention, and support from parents and teachers as do disabled children.

What Teachers Can Do

The introduction of a disabled child into the classroom may lead many teachers to feel they can no longer give an adequate amount of time to each student, and worry that this lack of direct instruction and guidance could increase the likelihood of problems or difficulties. Teachers need to be patient with students who have disabilities, and understand that these students may become upset when they cannot complete a task as well as a peer. It is important that teacher model a calm demeanor when confronting stress in the classroom. Otherwise, all the students will key in on the tension, and the group dynamic will deteriorate.

Teachers need to recognize that parents are important support persons in easing the stress that students feel. They need to find ways to make parents an extension of the classroom. In turn, teachers should offer support and comfort to parents as they deal with the stress associated with their child's disabilities. Children should receive help in learning to cope with stressful situations, both at school and at home.

Teachers need to be aware that because of family stress, children with disabilities are at a higher risk for being abused by a parent or another relative. Low-birthweight babies, for example, make up a significant number of abused children cases (Hunt & Marshall, 1994). Parents may have unrealistic expectations, or they may feel isolated from their extended families, increasing the likelihood that they may be unable to cope with the stress and consequently take out their frustrations on the child.

Parent-child interactions can be significantly affected when the child has a disability, depending on each person's temperament. Parents may resent the additional time required to meet the needs of a disability, possibly leading to dislike for, and mistreatment of, the child. Mothers of young children with disabilities tend to take more of a dominant role in their interactions with their children than mothers of children without disabilities do. If the child cannot communicate effectively, the mother may have difficulty interpreting cues and responses (Hunt & Marshall, 1994).

Some families do not participate in activities planned by school personnel because they are embarrassed about having a disabled child or they expect the child to act inappropriately in these settings. Some parents may overcompensate for the child's disability by not making any demands on the child. The disabled child may become confused and not understand why he has rules and standards in one setting (at school) and not in another (at home), and this may compound the tension being felt.

Managing Stress at School and Home

Children with disabilities often thrive on structure. Therefore, any imbalance in the routine—either at home or school—can be very upsetting for the disabled child. The school day is designed such that children must undergo a number of transitions while in attendance. Disabled children learn the order of the routines in their lives and usually keep consistent patterns that are necessary each day to satisfy those with whom they are interacting. Any break in the routine or change in procedures can upset the flow between academic subjects or between settings within the classroom or school building. Furthermore, expectations should be realistic and detailed—the child needs to know what to do and when. It is important for the teaching staff and the parents to be in communication so that each knows what standards are being set and what the child can or cannot achieve. When establishing the rules and routines that will help alleviate stress for the child with disabilities, uniformity between school and home is critical.

Life for children with disabilities is difficult, especially when they are unable to understand or discuss what is causing the difficulty. The child and the family have to deal with the everyday pressures of school while learning to cope with their disability and to make necessary adjustments. They must establish routines, and learn how to apply the skills learned in one arena to others.

Many children with disabilities have experienced academic and social problems for so long that they have become accustomed to being unsuccessful. A child who believes she cannot please the adults in her life may develop learned helplessness and become totally dependent on others. The child may shy away from trying new things in class for fear of failure. At home, she may resist volunteering to help with chores, because she is afraid that the effort will not be appreciated.

Children with disabilities often fail to develop a sense of self-direction and self-efficacy, and therefore may find many school events to be stressful in ways that their nondisabled peers do not. Overall, the disabled student often experiences a greater level of stress (Geisthardt & Munsch, 1996).

School-related stress is the most prevalent, untreated cause of academic failure today. Rubenzer (1988) reported that approximately 12 percent of the children with disabilities in the schools of the United States are at risk for developing stress-related problems. This stress may only increase as the child progresses through the various grade levels. For children with disabilities, the goals and objectives of an Individualized Educational Program (IEP) become more specific and more difficult as they progress. Stress management programs become necessary for every school.

A child who is being negatively affected by school-related stress can disrupt an entire classroom and the whole family (Hallowell & Ratey, 1994). In today's education environment, disabled children are included in regular classes. Thus, any disruptions—academic or otherwise—that involve the disabled child will also involve the classmates of that child. Children may not know how to act appropriately in response, further exacerbating the stress.

Children with disabilities, like anyone else, have hopes and dreams for their futures. They may become bitter witnessing their peers reaching certain milestones (e.g., going to school dances, graduating, getting a driver's license) that may be much more difficult, if not impossible, for them to attain. A child's capacity for hope may be virtually erased by the time the family seeks professional help (Hallowell & Ratey, 1994).

Understanding and Assisting the Parent

Parents of disabled children often have lives that are filled with uncertainty. It may be difficult to establish a routine, especially if the child is hyperactive. Keeping up with the disabled child's needs can be draining, as is maintaining a schedule of appointments with teachers, physicians, and counselors. Trying to meet all the needs of the disabled child can leave parents with little time for themselves or for other members of the family. Coping strategies, lifestyle changes, and stress-reduction exercises may help parents overcome these difficulties.

Coping strategies that may benefit parents include learning to prioritize activities, setting realistic goals, using positive self-talk, and scheduling time for playful activities. Lifestyle changes can involve time management, eating and sleeping properly, and learning to identify and anticipate family stressors. Keeping a daily journal may provide clues about what factors trigger stress in both the disabled child and the parents (Dillon, 1992).

The extent to which parents are able to cope with stressful situations depends on several factors (Leyser & Dekel, 1991): 1) the family's personal resources, financial and otherwise; 2) the family's internal resources, such as the role each family member plays in maintaining relationships; and 3) the support available from relatives, neighbors, and community organizations. It takes time and hard work, but a lower level of stress can be attained by learning coping strategies and taking advantage of all available support.

Professional services, including early intervention programs, can help parents. One effective model, first used in Wisconsin (Bright & Hayward, 1997), involves trained teachers visiting a home and demonstrating effective instructional practices for the parents. Parents learn to carry out lessons designed to meet their child's specific needs. These programs create an alliance between the school and home, as well as a supportive relationship between the teacher and the parent. These programs also may reduce stress, increase the family's coping skills, and improve relationships within the family (Bright & Hayward, 1997). By being a part of their child's development and education, the parents become more comfortable with the needs of the child. The parents then begin to accept and appreciate their child's abilities.

Understanding and Assisting the Child

As a result of delayed, or lowered, cognitive development, some children with disabilities tend to lack the appropriate coping skills to deal with stress. Children with disabilities may have difficulty even recognizing that they have a problem and need help.

Children with a disability need to be trained to use problem-solving or stress-reduction skills, such as learning to rely on peer support. They also may need to learn self-control, and to develop positive yet realistic views of their capabilities (Large, 1999).

Teachers and parents need to build a "safety net" for children with disabilities, if they are to help these children cope effectively with the challenges and stress in their lives. Such safety nets are built from:

- A healthy relationship with at least one parent or adult
- Well-developed social skills
- Well-developed problem-solving skills
- The ability to act independently
- A sense of positive self-esteem
- The ability to focus attention on an activity. (DeBord, 1996)

It is the responsibility of all the adults in a child's life to be teaching and reinforcing these skills. Children who live and work in supportive environments are more likely to develop adequate coping skills and become more hopeful about themselves and about their situations.

Useful Stress-Reduction Techniques

Does all this mean that the role of the teacher is more complex than it already is? Does this mean that the curriculum has one more area to be addressed?

In one sense, stress reduction techniques could be incorporated throughout the curriculum and for all students. Teachers should be looking for that teachable moment to demonstrate how to react in a time of stress. Whenever possible, teachers can introduce and/or reinforce coping strategies.

Children first need to be taught how to recognize stress and its associated symptoms. Begin by defining stress and showing how it affects the body. Teachers can explain how stress may bring on physiological changes, such as increased heart rate and muscular pain (Jackson & Owens, 1999). Strategies to combat stress can be taught once the children understand what stress is and can recognize its symptoms. The following are some of those strategies:

- Identify the source of stress
- Practice deep breathing and muscle relaxation techniques
- Play relaxing and calming music
- Dim the lighting
- Engage in a physical activity before studying
- Participate in "rap sessions," using communication skills
- Paint or draw when feeling tense. (Jackson & Owens, 1999)

Teachers also can reduce stress by breaking down assignments into smaller tasks.

Teachers need to be aware that children with disabilities differ greatly in their resilience to stressful situations. Some studies indicate that, for reasons that are unclear, boys are more prone to stress than girls. One possible explanation is the societal expectation for boys to act brave and strong, and not to cry when distressed (Katz, 1989). The teacher can communicate to the children that it is acceptable to react in certain ways. Teachers should teach some positive ways to express feelings. It is all right to feel angry, scared, or lonely, and children can learn to express those feelings in healthy ways.

Teachers can model how to react to stress. Children will learn good coping skills, for example, if they see teachers remaining calm in an emergency. They then will be more likely to cope positively with their own difficulties (Katz, 1989).

Teachers should offer sincere praise on a regular basis. This encouragement will help the disabled child to achieve both academically and socially, and will show him that someone cares. Cooperative, not competitive, activities are great for teaching trust and social skills.

Teachers should avoid putting unnecessary additional pressure on the disabled child, and instead set realistic goals and standards for achievement (Johnson, 1991). There may be times when it is important to work with the parents or a school counselor to develop a plan for reducing the stress. A support group within the school setting could include teachers, the school nurse, or a coach. Outside the school setting, social workers, therapists, or clergy could help.

Family counseling can allow everyone to better understand ways to help the disabled child through times of stress. The counselor can draw the family's attention to their strengths and to available social support, while teaching coping skills to the parents and the disabled child.

Conclusion

Although it is impossible to free children's lives of stressors, we can try to teach children to anticipate and cope with them. Simply taking action can bring relief (DeBord, 1996).

As adults, we can make sure we do not add to the children's level of stress by expecting them to act maturely before they are ready to do so. We should not expect a disabled learner to master the curriculum at the same pace that a nondisabled child can. We should not set goals that are too high or that will take too long to achieve. Instead, we can use praise to highlight the child's successes, and adopt a positive attitude about the child's work overall. We can help children identify and manage their feelings and reactions to stress. We show fairness in realizing that all children are unique and have particular needs. We can be patient and honest with each child. Above all, we can help children to like themselves, and we can teach with love and caring.

References

Bright, Jenifer A., & Hayward, Peter. (1997). Dealing with chronic stress: Coping strategies, self-esteem, and service use in mothers of handicapped children. *Journal of Mental Health, 6*(1), 67-74.

Cable, Edward. (1994). *Stress management for AD/HD parents.* Littleton, CO: The Colorado Advisory Network.

DeBord, Karen. (1996). *Helping children cope with stress.* Raleigh, NC: North Carolina Cooperative Extension Service. National Network for Child Care - NNCC.

Dillon, Kathleen M. (1992). Popping sealed air-capsules to reduce stress. *Psychological Reports, 71,* 243-246.

Geisthardt, Cheryl, & Munsch, Joyce. (1996). Coping with school stress: A comparison of adolescents with and without learning disabilities. *Journal of Learning Disabilities, 29*(3), 287-297.

Hallowell, Edward M., & Ratey, James J. (1994). *Driven to distraction.* New York: Simon & Schuster.

Hunt, Nancy, & Marshall, Kathleen. (1994). *Exceptional children and youth.* Boston: Houghton Mifflin.

Jackson, James T., & Owens, James L. (1999). A stress management classroom tool for teachers of children with BD. *Intervention in School and Clinic, 35*(2), 74-81.

Johnson, Cynthia E. (November 1991). *Helping your child deal with stress.* Raleigh, NC: North Carolina Cooperative Extension Service, North Carolina State University. Publication #HE-371.

Kaplan, Paul S. (1996). *Pathways for exceptional children.* St. Paul, MN: West Publishing Company.

Katz, Lillian G. (1989). *Coping with stress.* Washington, DC: Office of Educational Research and Improvement, U.S. Department of Education.

Kirk, Samuel A., & Gallagher, James J. (1989). *Educating exceptional children* (6th ed.). Boston: Houghton Mifflin.

Large, Rena. (1999). Easing the strain of students' stress. *NEA Today, 18*(1), 39-43.

Leyser, Yona, & Dekel, Gad. (1991). Perceived stress and adjustment in religious Jewish families with a child who is disabled. *Journal of Psychology Interdisciplinary & Applied, 125*(4), 427-439.

Margalit, Malka, & Ankonina, Dee B. (1991). Positive and negative affect in parenting disabled children. *Counseling Psychology Quarterly, 4*(4), 289-300.

National Information Center for Children and Youth With Disabilities. (1988). Children with disabilities: Understanding sibling issues. *NICHCY News Digest, Number 11.*

Rubenzer, Ronald L. (1988). *Stress management and the learning disabled.* (ERIC Document Reproduction Service No. ED295396)

Suggested Books

Arnold, L. Eugene. (1990). *Childhood stress.* New York: John Wiley & Sons. ISBN 0471508683.
This book examines aspects of psychosocial and biological stress, and covers the effect of stress on childhood development. It examines stressors specific to children and provides helpful coping mechanisms for teachers and parents.

Haggerty, Robert J. (Ed.). (1996). *Stress, risk, and resilience in children and adolescents: Processes, mechanisms, and interventions.* New York: Cambridge University Press. ISBN 0521576628.
This book is directed toward therapists, school counselors, teachers, and parents. It describes useful processes in helping children overcome stress.

Henderson, Nan, & Milstein, Mike M. (1996). *Resiliency in schools: Making it happen for students and educators.* Thousand Oaks, CA: Corwin Press. ISBN 0803963521.
This book traces the change in education and social services from a focus on deficits, problems, and risks, to the hopeful and inspiring news about resiliency—how young people and adults can bounce back from life's challenges.

Joseph, Joanne M., & Redlener, Irwin. (1994). *The resilient child: Preparing today's youth for tomorrow's world.* New York: Insight Books. ISBN 0306446464.
The authors explore ways to help children through stressful times, and describe the warning signs that indicate a need for professional help.

Krovetz, Martin L. (1999). *Fostering resiliency: Expecting all students to use their minds and hearts well.* Thousand Oaks, CA: Corwin Press. ISBN 0803966342.
Martin Krovetz provides concrete examples of schools that have developed resilient learning communities for both students and staff.

Kuczen, Barbara. (1987). *Childhood stress: How to raise a healthier, happier child.* New York: Dell Publishing Company. ISBN 0385295251.
This book offers parents and professionals information on the effects of stress in children and offers a blueprint for restoring a child's sense of safety and balance.

McCracken, Janet Brown. (1987). *Reducing stress in young children's lives.* Washington, DC: National Association for the Education of Young Children. ISBN 093598903x.
This book will help readers understand psychological trauma from a child's point of view; it also explores the ways both parents and professionals can help children heal.
Oehlberg, Barbara. (1996). *Making it better: Activities for children living in a stressful world.* St. Paul, MN: Redleaf Press. ISBN 1884834264.
This book is a collection of sensitive and caring activities. Teachers new to the field, as well as long-time veterans, will find the activities easy to implement.

Books About, and for, Children With Disabilities

Brown, Tricia, & Ortiz, Fran. (1995). *Someone special, just like you.* Toronto: Owlet Books. ISBN 0805042687.
This book shows preschool disabled students actively playing and learning.
Cairo, Shelley. (1988). *Our brother has Down's syndrome.* Willowdale, Ontario: Firefly Books. ISBN 0920303315.
A family story about Jai, a young child with Down's Syndrome. The book portrays his happy, busy life.
Fleming, Virginia, & Cooper, Floyd. (1993). *Be good to Eddie Lee.* New York: Philomel Books. ISBN 0399219935.
Christy learns to see the good qualities of Eddie Lee, a boy with Down's syndrome.
Klein, Lee, & Mauseth, Pam. (1994). *Are there stripes in heaven?* Mahwah, NJ: Paulist Press. ISBN 0809166186.
Patrick's sister Colleen, a Down's syndrome child, helps him to appreciate the simple joys of everyday experiences, including going to Mass and seeing their first rainbow.
Lasker, Joe. (1987). *He's my brother.* Niles, IL: Albert Whitman. ISBN 0807532185.
A young boy describes the experiences of his slow-learning younger brother.
Martin, Bill. (1999). *Knots on a rope.* Minneapolis, MN: Econo-Clad Books. ISBN 0613036077.
A grandfather uses a counting rope to help his blind grandson understand the passage of time, and helps the child face the challenge of blindness.
McKensie, Ellen Kindt. (1992). *Stargone John.* New York: Henry Holt. ISBN 0805020691.
Six-year-old John, emotionally withdrawn and resistant to traditional teaching methods, experiences ridicule and punishment at school. He is saved by a retired teacher who, despite her blindness, shares with John the world of reading and writing.
Muldoon, Kathleen. (1989). *Princess Pooh.* New York: Concept Books. ISBN 0807566276.
Jealous of what appears to be her invalid sister's royal treatment, Patty Jean tries using the wheelchair and discovers that having no choice but to use it is no fun at all.
Moon, Nicola. (1997). *Lucy's picture.* New York: Puffin Books. ISBN 0140557695.
A young girl creates a special picture that her blind grandfather can "see" with his hands.
Pascal, Francine. (1993). *Won't someone help Anna?* New York: Bantam Skylark. ISBN 0553480561.
One of Wakefield's classmates begins to act strangely; no one knows why until a deaf girl helps the other students to understand their friend's mysterious behavior.
Rabe, Berniece. (1991). *Where's Chimpy?* Niles, NY: Albert Whitman. ISBN 0807589276.
A girl with Down's syndrome and her dad search for her stuffed monkey, and take the opportunity to review the day.
Thompson, Mary. (1996). *Andy and his yellow frisbee.* Rockville, MD: Woodbine House. ISBN 0933149832.
A new girl tries to be friends with Andy, an autistic boy who spends every recess alone, spinning a yellow frisbee under the watchful eye of his older sister.

Organizations

Anxiety Disorders Association of America (ADAA)
11900 Parklawn Drive, Suite 100
Rockville, MD 20852
301-231-8368

National Institute of Mental Health (NIMH)
Anxiety Disorders Education Program
5600 Fishers Lane, Room 7C-02
Rockville, MD 20857

The American Academy of Experts in Traumatic Stress
368 Veterans Memorial Highway
Commack, NY 11725
516-543-2217

Pamphlets

Materials on the following topics can be obtained from the Anxiety Disorders Association of America:

Post-Traumatic Stress Disorder
Generalized Anxiety Disorder
Anxiety Disorders in Children and Adolescents
Anxiety Disorders: Helping a Family Member
Anxiety Disorders and Medication

Videotapes

The hero who couldn't read. (1984). ABC-TV. (Learning Disabilities)
How difficult can this be? (1996). The F.A.T. City Workshop. PBS Video. (Learning Disabilities)
Look what you've done: Stories of hope and resilience. (1997). PBS Video. (Learning Disabilities and Self-Esteem)
This side is good. (1983). Filmmakers Library. (Speech Disorders)
Being there. (1979). Lorimar/CBS/Fox. (Mental Retardation)
Gaby: A true story. (1987). Tri-Star Pictures. (Physical Disabilities)
The silent world of Jim. (1974). Film Communicators. (Deafness)
Panic disorder: Stories of hope. (1994). Modern Talking Picture Services. (Emotional Disturbance)
ADHD in the Classroom. (1994). Guilford Publications. (Attention Deficit)

Chapter 5
Matching Teaching Methods to Learning Styles

Marc Mahlios

Mismatches between a teacher's instructional method and children's learning styles are a common source of children's stress and often thwart their efforts to learn. I will describe the experiences of two children to illustrate this point, and call attention to the more cognitive, rather than affective, roots of some children's stressful experiences. The learning style construct used in this analysis, field dependence (FD) theory, is based on the work of Witkin, Moore, Goodenough, and Cox (1977).

Educators frequently focus on the content of a learner's thoughts in relation to available knowledge. Goldstein and Blackman (1978) identified field dependence as one of the five most salient cognitive style constructs. Witkin et al.'s field dependence theory appears equally synchronous with the two principal metaphors of human learning that dominate the education literature today, namely what Sfard (1998) calls the acquisition and participation metaphors. FD theory affords a comprehensive framework for effectively connecting pupil learning, teaching, and curriculum matters within school settings.

Vignette One: Carl

Carl is an 11-year-old in the 6th grade of a suburban elementary school located in the midwestern United States. According to his teacher and the school psychologist, Carl is of low-average intelligence. His prior school experience has been largely positive, however, and he has managed to achieve mostly passing grades thus far. Carl is generally well-liked by his peers and teachers at school, and his father and stepmother are involved and supportive. Many of his teachers describe Carl as a friendly, outgoing, gregarious child; academically, however, he has difficulty learning abstract concepts (such as those in his science class, for example). As a result, Carl has begun to act in inappropriate and occasionally dysfunctional ways. His science teacher notes that Carl's frustration is most apparent when lessons go beyond the obvious, literal, and factual dimensions of a concept, skill, or procedure.

One of the instructional methods Carl's science teacher typically uses, the concept attainment model (Bruner, 1961), is common in science instruction. It requires students to identify essential attributes or characteristics of a concept and then apply those attributes in differentiating examples from non-examples of the concept under study. The methodology also requires students to reflect on the actual cognitive strategies they use in attempting to differentiate examples from non-examples of a concept as an aid to learning similar concepts and a basic inductive model of learning. The actual concept attainment strategy consists of three parts. In part one, the teacher presents examples of the concept under study (for example, class 1 levers). Examples are both positive (e.g., a seesaw) and negative (e.g., a wheelbarrow). Students are required to compare the characteristics (or attributes) of the examples to tease out the essential characteristics of the concept represented by the positive examples (in the example of "class 1 levers," the attributes are fulcrum, effort arm, and load arm). Once the students have correctly identified all of the essential characteristics of the concept, they use those characteristics to establish a definition of the concept. In part two, students identify additional positive examples (e.g., a crowbar) of the concept. Finally, in part three, students describe the metacognitive strategies they used in identifying the essential characteristics of the concept from the examples studied. Carl frequently becomes baffled and frustrated when asked to test hypotheses (from part two above).

Compounding his frustration and stress, his peers occasionally ridicule his inability to respond to the teacher's inquiries, exacerbating his feelings of failure. It is important to note that the instructional tasks that comprise teaching also provide students cognitive and social tasks that constitute learning strategies, which eventually become the framework for subsequent learning. In this example, as Carl's teacher uses the concept attainment strategy to teach the concept of levers she communicates to students that this inductive approach is an effective learning strategy. Most students eventually come to understand learning as an inductive process of categorizing information about ideas, based on distinguishable concept attributes. In this case, knowledge about the concept of class 1 levers (e.g., scissors) is based upon an inductive learning model that is demonstrated through the interaction of teacher-student-objects. The students learn that by contrasting and comparing examples, they can come to know the concept. Carl, however, achieves little success with this process; he is unable to discern all of the relevant attributes needed to identify a concept in an actual example.

Vignette Two: Holly

Holly is an 11-year-old in the 6th grade of a suburban elementary school in the midwestern United States. According to her teacher and the school psychologist, she is of above-average intelligence. Holly's prior school experience has been very positive and she has achieved mostly above-average grades. Although Holly is generally accepted by her peers and the teachers, she is not considered to be popular. Her parents are involved and supportive. Her teachers describe Holly as a perfectionist who pays a great deal of attention to detail and generally meets their highest expectations. After Holly was accepted into the school's gifted and talented program, however, she became worried about falling behind in her other classes and eventually withdrew from the program. In addition, Holly is a competitive gymnast who practices about 18 hours per week. Despite being a high-achieving student, Holly is uncomfortable in social academic learning settings (e.g., cooperative learning groups). Holly's teacher has remarked that Holly shows signs of being overly stressed—crying, for instance—when asked to join in cooperative, group-structured science lessons. Her science teacher notes that Holly is most likely to become frustrated with classroom activities that require her to deal with ambiguous and vague ideas, and when participating in groups that do not work together well and thus run the risk of not producing what Holly believes to be "what the teacher wants."

Holly's teacher typically uses a cooperative learning strategy, commonly used in science (and other content) instruction at the elementary school level. The model is based on the idea that student learning is best achieved through the process of social interaction with peers, and that knowledge is a social construct that issues from the negotiation of people in pursuit of a common goal (Johnson & Johnson, 1990; Slavin, 1990). A more recent view of constructivist learning and teaching principles (Phillips, 1995) states that students, through their participation in cooperative learning tasks, essentially are required to negotiate meaning and knowledge through socially mediated structures. Lave and Wenger (1991) describe this process of learning as a legitimate peripheral participation.

Central to the general framework of constructivism (Brooks & Brooks, 1993) is the idea that student learning is not merely the acquisition of intact information external to the learner, but rather each learner actively creates (i.e., constructs) knowledge from a dynamic interaction between oneself and the world. The social constructivist model presents learning in a social context as paramount; that is, people are social creatures, and so classrooms can function like mini-societies. In this social context, student learning is conceived of as a social participation metaphor (Sfard, 1998). One way that teachers can structure social learning activities for students is through cooperative learning instructional strategies (Johnson & Johnson, 1990).

In Holly's science class, the teacher asked small groups to identify some of the relationships between organisms in a water pond ecosystem. Multiple relationships can be identified, and the teacher will accept any credible hypothesis the groups produce. However, the students must "construct" and justify the relationship among variables in their hypothesis. Holly finds it difficult to learn this science concept when it is presented to her in such a fashion.

Source of the Stress Affecting Carl's and Holly's Learning

In the two cases described above, the students experienced considerable stress, although in different ways. The stress was caused primarily because their cognitive and social skills did not mesh well with the academic concepts they were required to learn, nor with the teacher's instructional method. Both students are capable of understanding the concepts being taught, and their study and work skills seem adequate. Both teachers used currently supported instructional practices (concept attainment and cooperative learning groups), yet in both situations a fundamental mismatch between instructional strategies and individual learning styles resulted in less than optimal learning outcomes and considerable stress.

By pursuing capitalization matches (Messick, 1976), the teachers could have reduced Carl's and Holly's stress and improved their chances for learning. The key idea in this process is to match individual students' differences with learning tasks and environments that draw on those differences. In our examples of Carl and Holly, the elements include Witkin's theory of field dependence (an individual difference) and instructional methods (concept attainment and cooperative learning groups).

Cognitive Style

Cognitive style refers to the psychological consistencies in a person's manner of acquiring, processing, and structuring information. Each learner's means of cognition differs, including such processes as perception, thought, memory, imagery, and problem solving. The notion of variations in one's style of cognition implies more than the degree of ability or skill in these cognitive processes; it means the existence of individual differences and preferences in gaining, storing, processing, structuring, and using information. In short, qualitative differences in mental functioning underlie the concept of cognitive style.

It is important to recognize that cognitive style differences do not necessarily relate to differences in intellectual ability. Rather, a person's cognitive style is one element in a larger set of cognitive abilities and processes. Depending on the context in which a task is undertaken, cognitive style can either enhance or hinder one's performance. In other words, a particular cognitive style is not inherently good or bad; its success instead depends on the task and context in which one functions. How professional educators respond to these differences when designing curriculum, selecting instructional methods, and structuring the learning environment can significantly affect students' learning and development. Teachers can alleviate students' stress and help them learn by being aware of how different teaching methods match up with different learning styles.

Field dependence theory refers to the extent to which a person is able to perceive parts of a field as discrete from the surrounding field as a whole, or to the extent to which the field's organization determines one's ability to perceive its components. Cognitive style measures such as field dependence may help educators understand how students deal with symbolic representations, solve problems, and comprehend complex materials, and even help explain why students choose one academic track (e.g., mathematics or sociology) over another.

Field-dependent students such as Carl are more likely to experience difficulty with academic problems wherein the solution depends on taking some critical element out of its context. Carl's cognitive style limits his ability to perceive the attributes of a concept (e.g., of a class 1 lever in physics) in differing contexts; thus, he has trouble identifying the attributes of one similar example from another (e.g., a shovel and a screwdriver). In short, Carl needs to see things contextually to understand how to solve particular problems.

Field-independent students, such as Holly, are better able to overcome the dominant organization of the field, or to restructure it if the field lacks inherent organization. Holly's case, however, illustrates that such learners can be uncomfortable functioning in a social context when solving a particular problem (e.g., determining the relationship between organisms in an ecosystem) for which multiple hypotheses exist, and one solution is to be derived from group processes that favor knowledge construction over knowledge discovery and acquisition. Holly is much more successful when she can solve problems analytically, and rely on the teacher as the source for testing her hypothesis.

Holly's preferred cognitive strategy is what Bruner called the "active hypothesis testing" model (e.g., "Is a wheel barrow an example of a class 1 lever according to the concept or rule?"). The student is said to have learned a concept when he or she can actively test the hypothesis (in and out of context) and when the teacher confirms it as tenable. In this model, unfounded hypotheses are discarded. Field-independent persons also learn concepts through cue salience, which means that students will go beyond the apparent array of stimulus cues (concept attributes) to identify concepts in unfamiliar contexts. In contrast, field-dependent students need greater clarity of the cues in a learning context in order to learn the nature of a concept, and they need greater assistance in generalizing and applying useful clues from one context to another, especially when they lack similarity.

Teaching and Learning Options

American educators have struggled to identify and successfully implement practical ways to respond to individual students' myriad differences (Brophy & Good, 1974) (e.g., intellectual ability, gender, race, personality characteristics, and individual behaviors). More recently, as a consequence of inclusive education programs, teachers need approaches to address the different needs of children with various disabilities. This most recent trend creates an additional challenge for regular classroom teachers as they strive to adapt and differentiate approaches to curriculum and teaching across an increasingly broad range of means (Wang & Lindvall, 1984).

While the larger debate about the ideas inherent in "inclusive education" and its practices is far from settled, it is increasingly clear that the gap between these ideas and how individual classroom practitioners will respond to this expanded set of individual pupil differences has widened, leading to considerable teacher responsibilities (and stress!). With few exceptions, teachers do not have enough strategies at their disposal to meet this enhanced responsibility (Sindelar, 1995). One effective method involves matching models.

Messick (1976) proposed four types of matching models for use in teaching: 1) corrective matches, in which teaching models rectify learner deficiencies in critical skills; 2) compensatory matches, in which teaching approaches compensate for pupil limitations by providing organizing structures the student is unable to provide herself; 3) challenge matches (mismatches), in which a conflict is created between elements of instruction and pupil characteristics so as to challenge the pupil (based upon a Piagetian disequilibrium notion); and 4) capitalization matches (preferential matches), in which the instructional models used with students draw on their inherent strengths, resulting in preferred modes of functioning. Studies demonstrating student learning under different types of matches have been conducted by Mahlios (1990) and Saracho (1990).

Can the insights provided above help us answer the question, "Why are Carl and Holly having difficulty learning science concepts when presented to them in these commonly used instructional meth-

Table 1
Messick's Matching Models

Type of Match	Instructional Method	Cognitive Style
1) Corrective	Cooperative Learning Groups	Field Independent
2) Compensatory	Advance Organizer	Field independent
3) Challenge	Concept Attainment	Field Dependent
4) Capitalization	Group Investigation	Field Dependent

odologies (concept attainment and cooperative learning groups)?" One could answer that although the methodology each teacher selected was professionally "correct," the students nevertheless were being confronted with a fundamental mismatch to their cognitive skills. For Carl, it appears that the use of more social models of instruction (e.g., cooperative learning groups) would more effectively tap his cognitive strengths, while the reverse seems true for Holly.

Some viable strategies can be employed to effectively respond to students' varied learning needs and styles. Two strategies are particularly salient to Carl's and Holly's cases. The first method (Hunt, 1970) involves deliberately mismatching a pupil and the learning environment, in an effort to move the learner toward an enhanced state of cognitive complexity. Under Hunt's scheme, for example, Carl would be considered to function at a "low complexity" level of information processing. He tends to approach learning of concepts as an "either/or" phenomenon; that is, he does not typically discriminate among the elements of a concept in a finely graduated manner. The optimal learning environment for Carl, under Hunt's model, is highly structured—one that allows (indeed requires) Carl to actually discriminate among stimuli and allow for some "gray" areas. Thus, while Carl's learning environment would match his cognitive style, it also would require him to move up to the next level of cognitive complexity.

Over time, Carl would be helped to achieve a more complex cognitive system, or structure, for processing information and seeing alternative relationships among concepts. Under this scenario, Carl's teacher can create a deliberate mismatch in order to actively promote Carl's intellectual and academic growth. In this scheme, some degree of stress is beneficial, and thus justifiable.

Carl's current level of cognitive complexity is relatively low. Initially, Carl's teacher needs to provide him with clear-cut examples of the three lever categories (e.g., class 1, a crowbar; class 2, a wheelbarrow; class 3, a broom). He can be provided additional simple drawings of lever objects and asked to place the objects in their respective categories. Once Carl has achieved a reasonable level of success with this category sorting task, his teacher can ask Carl to identify, in each category example, the three elements that are common to all concept levels (e.g., fulcrum, effort, and load), and to show where each of these elements is found within the examples that he already had categorized. So, for example, once Carl successfully places new examples of levers into the three categories, he can be given the task (probably best handled in a small work group) of correctly locating and labeling the fulcrum, effort, and load elements in each new example presented to him and his work group. This second step requires Carl to extend his cognitive complexity by successfully categorizing each new example, and locating each example's three core concept attributes and showing their relationship to one another. This phase of locating and describing the fulcrum attribute in a wheelbarrow is a more complex task than simply categorizing a lever object (e.g., a broom as a class 3 lever).

Next, Carl's teachers would ask him to locate and then modify some real-life examples of lever objects. For instance, if Carl locates a teeter-totter on the school playground and successfully categorizes it as class 1 lever (locating the fulcrum, load, and effort), he might next be asked to manipulate the relationship among the attributes—to show how to lift a larger load while maintaining the same effort, for example. This cognitive task is much more complex than the first two and actually moves Carl toward the goal of needing to conceptualize relationships among the actual lever attributes in this example. Toward the end of the school year, Carl's teacher might begin to show him how to plot the values for the three lever attributes on a graph.

In this scenario, Carl's teacher carefully creates a slight mismatch between Carl's cognitive complexity and the academic task he is attempting to learn. Even though Carl will struggle to understand a slightly higher level of task complexity and although this process will likely produce in Carl some level of stress, the stress will be manageable and it will stimulate his intellectual growth.

Holly would be considered a student of "moderately high complexity" on Hunt's scale. Her optimal learning environment would be one in which she would be simultaneously responsible for attaining a learning goal, while contributing to a group learning situation. Holly prefers to problem-solve alone and in a deductive framework. In order to advance her cognitive development, however, the learning environment should contain elements of cooperative learning.

Holly's current level of cognitive complexity is moderately high. She is easily able to categorize examples of levers into the three classes and correctly isolate the lever attributes. When working in a group, however, she finds it difficult to share her knowledge with other students or to help them understand her reasoning. One way Holly's teacher can create the desired mismatch between her current cognitive level and classroom learning tasks is through assessment activities in the levers and pulley unit. First, the teacher could ask Holly to "think aloud" as she categorizes an example (lever classes 1, 2, 3); correctly locates example attributes (e.g., the fulcrum in a screwdriver); and explains how she actually reasons through these examples. Second, Holly could be charged to work with other cognitively complex students to prepare some assessment problems using material from the classroom lab. The intention would be to have Holly interact substantively and socially with her peers as they create and represent a problem as an assessment task for other students. In effect, this task will stretch Holly intellectually and socially, a process that may help move her to the next level of cognitive complexity. The Full Option Science System (FOSS) (1993) materials contain excellent examples of assessment activities and materials that Holly and her teacher could use to organize and carry out these tasks.

Conclusions

Hunt's framework of a carefully designed mismatch between pupils and their learning tasks can enhance their cognitive growth. Increased levels of cognitive complexity are achieved through alterations in classroom learning environments, including teaching strategies.

Bruce Joyce and his colleagues (Joyce, Weil, & Calhoun, 2000) argue that by using various instructional strategies, teachers are, in effect, helping students learn by forcing them to see things from different perspectives. In other words, while it is commonly thought that "teachers teach" and "students learn," teachers can help students learn to learn in varied ways in response to the forms of teaching provided them (e.g., through cooperative learning groups, concept attainment, direct instruction, lectures, non-directive teaching, and so on) (Joyce et al., 2000). Carl would benefit from having information presented to him in a carefully sequenced, deductive fashion (e.g., teacher presentations as in Ausubel, 1968; or direct instruction as in Rosenshine, 1970). The concepts need to be carefully sequenced in a hierarchical fashion, beginning with broad, abstract concepts that lead to more narrow and concrete concepts. Holly could profit from the so-called social models of teaching (e.g., descriptions of metacognitive processes in her learning, group investigation, cooperative learning groups, role playing, and so on) as a means of helping her acquire social constructivism learning strategies (see, for example, Vygotsky, 1986). Like Carl, Holly can be taught learning strategies that are integral to the teaching methodologies commonly used in elementary classrooms.

At first glance, the strategies suggested in this chapter may seem contradictory. It has been suggested throughout this chapter that a fundamental mismatch between a student's learning style and the learning environment leads to stress and inhibits learning. Many learning theorists (e.g., Piaget, 1960) point out, however, that real intellectual growth is associated with a certain degree of learner discomfort. In other words, if they are too comfortable with the present state of their learning and teaching relationship, students will be less motivated to actually advance their intellectual capacity and functioning. The complex task for teachers is to gauge the relative degree of match and mismatch between the pupils' characteristics and the learning environment created in order to maximize learning, without creating undue or counterproductive stress. In the cases of Carl and Holly, the match created between their learning styles and the larger classroom learning environment was outside of this optimal range and thus was dysfunctional, resulting in excessive stress for each of them. The strategies suggested here can help their teachers create more optimal learning contexts. This optimal match can be achieved only by well-prepared professional teachers who systematically plan and adjust their teaching based on the unique characteristics of their students and the common elements of the local schooling context.

The temptation exists to make broad generalizations about the relative worth of certain approaches to teaching without knowledge of how these procedures are likely to affect specific students. This must be avoided. It is the appropriate application of an instructional approach that is sought, rather than any single approach. Consideration of the particular context and of the student's characteristics must also be paramount. What may prove most useful is a careful selection of instructional strategies that promote children's development in "optimally stressful" ways (see, for example, Dewey's (1916) notion of disequilibrium).

Unfortunately, teachers frequently encounter barriers, largely a function of time constraints and the range of student variability, in responding to individual student differences like the ones described above. Now that most schools use computers, they could be used to provide the kinds of sought-after instructional matches to learners' difference (Desberg & Fisher, 1989) now found in most schools. Several examples of computer applications in support of teaching and learning can be found at the University of Kansas Web site, the High Plains Regional Technology in Education Consortium (www.hprtec.org). One model found at this Web site, "Trackstar" (trackstar.hprtec.org) is an on-line interface that helps teachers integrate Web sites into their actual teaching. Another tool, called "PROFILER" (www.profiler.hprtec.org), enriches instruction by creating collaboration between teachers and students around specific learning tasks. Finally, the KanCRN site (www.kancrn.org) offers teachers and their students opportunities to participate in actual ongoing research projects with university scientists. Data gathered at local school and community locations is transferred on-line to researchers at universities across the United States for inclusion in their studies. Two additional sites specifically geared toward providing instruction in response to students' individual differences are the On-Line Academy (www.onlineacademy.edu) and the Center for Research on Learning (www.ku-crl.org).

While we would not want all, or even most, instruction to take place between a computer and students, the potential for this technology to help teachers accommodate the wise range of learning styles in the classroom is clear. Similarly, they afford the ability to test children on various cognitive style dimensions. These measures all hold promise for better utilizing our instructional resources and better supporting students' learning efforts.

REFERENCES

Ausubel, David. (1968). *Educational psychology: A cognitive view.* New York: Holt, Rinehart and Winston.

Brooks, Jacqueline Grennon, & Brooks, Martin G. (1993). *In search of understanding: The case for constructivist classrooms.* Alexandria, VA: Association for Supervision and Curriculum Development.

Brophy, Jere, & Good, Tom. (1974). *Teacher-student relationships: Causes and consequences.* New York: Holt, Rinehart and Winston.

Bruner, Jerome. (1961). *The process of education.* Cambridge, MA: Harvard University Press.

Desberg, Paul, & Fisher, Carl. (1989). *Teaching with technology.* Boston: Allyn and Bacon Interactive.

Dewey, John. (1916). *Democracy and education.* New York: Macmillan.

Full Option Science System (FOSS). (1993). *Levers and pulleys.* University of California, Encyclopedia Britannica Educational Corporation, Chicago: IL.

Goldstein, Kenneth M., & Blackman, Sheldon. (1978). *Cognitive style: Five approaches and relevant research.* New York: John Wiley & Sons.

Hunt, David E. (1970). A conceptual level matching model for coordinating learner characteristics with educational approaches. *Interchange: A Journal of Educational Studies, 1*(2), 1-31.

Johnson, David W., & Johnson, Robert T. (1990). *Cooperation and competition: Theory and research.* Edina, MN: Interaction Book Co.

Joyce, Bruce, Weil, Marsha, & Calhoun, Emily. (2000). *Models of teaching.* Boston: Allyn and Bacon.

Lave, Jean, & Wenger, Etienne. (1991). *Situated learning: Legitimate peripheral participation.* Cambridge, UK: Cambridge University Press.

Mahlios, Marc. (1990). The influence of cognitive style on the teaching practices of elementary teachers. *Early Child Development and Care, 51,* 89-107.

Messick, Samuel. (1976). *Individuality in learning.* San Francisco: Jossey-Bass.

Piaget, Jean. (1960). *The child's conception of the world.* Atlantic Highlands, NJ: Humanities Press.

Phillips, Denis C. (1995). The good, the bad and the ugly: The many faces of constructivism. *Educational Researcher, 24*(7), 5-12.

Rosenshine, Barak. (1970). The stability of teacher effects upon student achievement. *Review of Educational Research, 40,* 647-662.

Saracho, Olivia N. (1990). *Cognitive style and early education.* London: Gordon and Breach Science Publishers.

Sfard, Anna. (1998). On two metaphors for learning and the dangers of choosing just one. *Educational Researcher, 27,* 4-13.

Sindelar, Paul T. (1995). Full inclusion of students with learning disabilities and its implications for teacher education. *Journal of Special Education, 29,* 234-244.

Slavin, Robert E. (1990). *Cooperative learning: Theory, research, and practice.* Englewood Cliffs, NJ: Prentice Hall.

Vygotsky, Lev S. (1986). *Thought and language* (rev. ed.). Cambridge, MA: MIT Press.

Wang, Margaret C., & Lindvall, Mauritz C. (1984). Individual differences and school learning environments. In E. W. Gordon (Ed.), *Review of research in education* (Vol. 11, pp. 161-226). Washington, DC: American Educational Research Association.

Witkin, Herman A., Moore, Carol A., Goodenough, Donald R., & Cox, Patricia W. (1977). Field-dependent and field-independent cognitive styles and their educational implications. *Review of Educational Research, 47,* 1-64.

RESOURCES FOR TEACHERS

Davey, Beth, & Menke, Deborah. (1990). The importance of cognitive style in children's acquisition of reading skill. In O. Saracho (Ed.), *Cognitive style in early education* (pp. 79-84). London: Gordon and Breach Science Publishers.

Dunn, Rita, Dunn, Kenneth, & Perrin, Janet. (1994). *Teaching young children through their individual learning styles: Practical approaches for grades K-12.* Boston: Allyn and Bacon.

Full Option Science System (FOSS). (1993). *Levers and pulleys.* University of California, Encyclopedia Britannica Educational Corporation, Chicago: IL.

Hale-Benson, Janice E. (1986). *Black children: Their roots, culture, and learning styles.* Baltimore: Johns Hopkins University Press.

Hunt, David, E. (1970). A conceptual level matching model for coordinating learner characteristics with educational approaches. *Interchanges, 1*(3), 68-82.

Hunt, David E., & Sullivan, Edmund V. (1974). *Between psychology and education.* Hinsdale, IL: Dryden.

Kogan, Nathan, & Saarni, Carolyn. (1990). Cognitive styles in children: Some evolving trends. In

O. Saracho (Ed.), *Cognitive style in early education* (pp. 3-31). London: Gordon and Breach Science Publishers.
Kogan, Nathan. (1976). *Cognitive styles in infancy and early childhood.* Hillsdale, NJ: Lawrence Erlbaum Associates.
Mahlios, Marc. (1981). Instructional design and cognitive styles of teachers in elementary schools. *Perceptual and Motor Skills, 52,* 335-338.
Mamchur, Carolyn. (1996). *A teacher's guide to cognitive theory and learning style.* Alexandria, VA: Association for Supervision and Curriculum Development.
Messick, Samuel. (1984). The nature of cognitive styles: Problems and promise in educational practice. *Educational Psychologist, 19*(2), 59-74.
Rayner, Richard, & Rayner, Stephen, R. (1998). *Cognitive styles and learning strategies: Understanding style differences in learning behaviour.* London: D. Fulton Publishers.
Saracho, Olivia. (1991). Teacher expectations and cognitive style: Implications for students' academic achievement. *Early Child Development and Care, 77,* 97-108.
Shipman, Stephanie, & Shipman, Virginia C. (1979; 1985). Cognitive styles: Some conceptual, methodological, and applied issues. In E. W. Gordon (Ed.), *Review of research in education* (Vol. 12, pp. 229-291). Washington, DC: American Educational Research Association.
Witkin, Herman A., & Goodenough, Donald. (1981). *Cognitive styles: Essence and origin.* New York: International Universities Press.

Resources for Parents

Block, Jack, Kogan, Nathan, & Block, Jeunne H. (1998). Parental teaching and children's cognitive style. *International Journal of Educational Research, 29,* 187-204.
Olson, Sheryl, Bates, John E., & Bayles, Kathryn. (1984). Mother-infant interactions and the development of individual differences in children's cognitive competence. *Developmental Psychology, 20,* 166-179.
Laosa, Luis M., & Sigel, Irving E. (Eds.). (1982). *Families as learning environments for children.* New York: Plenum Press.
Wapner, Seymour, & Demick, Jack. (Eds.). *Field dependence-independence: Cognitive style across the life span.* Hillsdale, NJ: Lawrence Earlbaum Associates.

Helpful Web sites

KanCRN: www.kancrn.org
Kansas University Center for Research on Learning: www.ku-crl.org
On-Line Academy: www.onlineacademy.edu
PROFILER: www.profiler.hprtec.org
High Plains Regional Technology in Education Consortium: www.hprtec.org

PART II

Stress: Adult Roles

Chapter 6
Mediating Stress: Personal Growth for Student Teachers

Gail McEachron

Billy was not like the other 5th-graders. He seemed older and wise to the world. In the beginning he seemed suspicious of me, which made me, in turn, somewhat suspicious of him. And this is how we began, an adult and a 5th-grader who seemed set to prove something to each other. As a first-year teacher, I wanted to prove to Billy that I cared about him. I wanted to teach him about the joy of learning. Having just completed a teacher preparation program, I was full of enthusiasm about what I had learned about children and youth. I didn't know what he wanted.

Billy didn't interact very much with the other children in the class. He set himself apart and kept to himself inside the classroom. Two classroom activities, however, brought out a rare animation in Billy—science activities, and when I read My Side of the Mountain *by Jean Craighead George. The science activities were always experimental in nature, and Billy was particularly enthralled by manipulating batteries and bulbs, and any other wiring activities. He loved experimenting in general, and positively effervesced when making closed circuits. As I read* My Side of the Mountain, *I would see Billy looking up from his desk—something he seldom did. It was almost as if he were caught off guard, and I knew that Billy was captivated by the adventures of Sam, the main character. Beyond the appeal of adventure, however, Billy himself seemed informed about falcons. Terminology like "talons" and "quiver," which were beyond the life experiences of most of the other students, came easily to him. I made a mental note to find out if he had ever gone hunting.*

I was surprised when I received an invitation to Billy's birthday party. The neighborhood where Billy lived was about 45 minutes away from my apartment. Making the commute on a Saturday for any other reason would not appeal to me. As a 22-year-old, weekends were an opportunity to be with my "adult" friends. But I saw Billy's invitation as more than a birthday party invitation; it was an opportunity to be let in on all the unanswered questions. It was a possible sign that he wanted to open up more. So I went, and I had a great time!

How things took a turn for the worse is still hazy for me. I don't know how our communication patterns became more indirect, but maybe they always were. Billy and I would connect through science or literature or a birthday party; unlike my interactions with some of the other 5th-graders, however, we never had more informal chats. Billy was not comfortable with small talk. Unfortunately, Billy and I went from the unspoken connection to the abyss. Here is how a caring relationship became estranged.

The 5th-grade classes set up intramurals for baseball. Teams competed until the two teams with the best records played each other in a series of games. Soon, the tension was building. My 5th-grade class was one of the finalists, and Billy was one of the key players. But the "jocks" were coming to me with complaints about Billy's unsportsmanlike conduct. They said that Billy would listen to me, so naturally I wanted to do anything I could to keep things in perspective. Sports hysteria was something I never had experienced, and so the discussion seemed rather matter-of-fact from my standpoint. I told Billy, "Sportsmanship is an important part of the game, in addition to physical skill and strategy, and if name-calling and harassment of the players on the opposing team continues, it will be necessary to sit out of the game for a period of time." So what was the big deal?

For some reason, the rivalry intensified and Billy's behavior not only did not improve, it worsened. Doing my teacherly thing, setting an example, following through, and so on, I asked Billy to sit out for part of the next game. Because of complaints from teachers and students about Billy's behavior, I felt obliged to take disciplinary action. Disciplining Billy was a new dimension of our relationship, one that didn't seem to fit with the way we "understood" each other.

The next morning when I got to school, I learned that Billy had taken a BB gun and shot out all the windows of a church. In addition, it turned out he was on probation from the juvenile authorities (which was news to me). The shooting meant that he would be returned to a juvenile detention home. When I called his mother to find out more of the details, she was not very coherent. She called to her husband to speak with me. When he refused, I could hear her recriminating him. The father never came to the phone, and I didn't have any further communication with Billy's parents.

In the days ahead, I occasionally passed Billy's younger brother in the hallway; it broke my heart to see him because he looked just like Billy. I would ask about Billy, and the younger boy would say he was doing "ok." I never saw Billy again. I had failed miserably in my goal to prove to him that I cared about him and to teach the joy of learning.

Twenty-five years is a long time to grieve over the loss of a student, but I still feel as intensely about what happened during that first year of teaching as if it were yesterday. Movies such as *Lean on Me* and *Stand and Deliver* tend to sensationalize the experiences between teachers and students (Joseph & Burnaford, 1994). Unraveling the true depth of the losses and emotional pain, however, is not easily portrayed in a feature length film.

Looking back, I would have done many things differently if I had them to do all over again; unfortunately, we cannot undo our mistakes. Consequently, I believe that Billy remains with me as a reminder that being placed in charge of other people's children brings certain risks and responsibilities that can be overwhelming. Perhaps his appearance in this chapter will forewarn novice teachers about those risks and responsibilities, and the associated stress. Often, the situations they face are difficult and do not make sense; and there are no guaranteed solutions.

Young children enliven the classroom with such sparkling qualities as spontaneity, joy, affection, innocence, and wonder at the ways of the world. Many novice teachers were drawn to the profession by these characteristics, as well as by a desire to offer guidance and nurturance. Working with young children is often believed to be less stressful than teaching young adolescents. Novice teachers rarely consider the stress that even very young children face, or the stress that they themselves will face as a result.

Novice teachers should prepare themselves for the possibility of unexpected and often unpleasant events, and expect to experience the full range of emotions as their charges experience neglect, separation, trauma, poverty, and conflict. Children who are experiencing stress in their lives express their needs in ways that often create stress for those around them. Having observed student teachers for 25 years, I have gained some insights into how this stress is manifested in the classroom and how student teachers often respond to these socially challenging situations. The interaction of these forces either contributes to the growth for the individuals involved or creates additional stress for not only the individual children and the student teacher, but also for the classroom as a whole. Although stress factors will be underscored in the context of this book, it is important to point out that, for the student teachers, facing these issues is a healthy part of learning to be effective in the classroom. Learning to mediate one's own stress levels and conflict in the workplace is a necessary step toward being especially receptive to children who are struggling at home or school.

Can I Do It?

As a college professor teaching social studies and language arts, I meet students who are excited, curious, and anxious to expand their repertoire of teaching strategies. These courses are taught just prior to the student teaching experience, and they often include a field placement during which students have opportunities to try out some of the lessons they have designed. I have noticed a definite shift in the students' attentiveness when the discussions turn to hypothetical classroom situations that portray the children as less than enthusiastic about the carefully designed lesson plans. These discussions demonstrate that the preservice teachers are asking themselves, "Can I do it?" When things do not go well, preservice teachers naturally question whether or not they are really capable of teaching. Rather than seeing themselves as novices in need of further experience, the whole of teaching seems to be linked to the whole of their person. And they are right! Yet they do need additional experience before they can answer this question fairly.

Issues Facing the Novice Teacher

I am humbled when I watch one student teacher juggle the needs of 20 to 30 children. Most student teachers demonstrate continuous growth and build confidence as they come to understand the multidimensional nature of the teaching role. Others develop competence, yet still question whether or not the various teaching roles are for them. Some, far fewer in number, realize that they "can do it," but that teaching is not for them. And, typically, a couple of student teachers think they can be successful, but need help recognizing the mismatch between themselves, children, and the teaching profession.

Many factors mediate these patterns of adjustment: personal abilities; personality; the strengths of the teacher preparation program; school ethos; school faculty, staff, and administrators; parental involvement; student characteristics; the social climate toward the teaching profession (as influenced by federal, state, and local politics); and community issues, such as attitudes toward school prayer, second-language learning, charter schools, and so on. In keeping with the purpose of this book, the focus of this chapter is on student teacher characteristics, specifically the manner in which they mediate children's stress.

Both novice and experienced teachers must learn to mediate, cope with, and reduce stress. For the novice contemplating a commitment to the teaching profession, these are competencies that require growth, particularly during the student teaching internship and other practicum experiences. In order for that growth to take place, student teachers need to learn how to manage children's stress. Such stress can be carry-over from the home or community, or normal classroom stress that may or may not be tied to home situations. To illustrate the first scenario, a child may be upset from an argument that transpired at home over breakfast and consequently act out in some way at school—either being withdrawn or aggressive. How the student teacher responds to these carry-over stresses will either help the child work through this time or possibly add to the child's frustration.

To illustrate the second scenario, student teachers (and even experienced classroom teachers) may contribute to stress levels in the classroom as a result of the way they address situations. Children may be used to activities being structured in a certain way at home. When they find a match to that structure in the classroom, things tend to run more smoothly. Children may feel stressed, however, if they find themselves in a classroom environment that is structured and managed very differently than at home. For example, kindergartners and 1st-graders whose parents hang up their clothes for them may have difficulty in a classroom where they are encouraged and expected to take responsibility for storing their own belongings in a certain location each morning. Whether or not the child becomes stressed might depend on if he or she perceives the student teacher to be interacting in a negative way. Many of these situations reflect different styles of teaching and parenting that are equally valid.

Novices in Transition

The experiences of student teachers will be described in the following clusters. "Struggles Without Success: Not a Good Match" describes those who struggled and were not successful. "If At First You Don't Succeed" describes those who needed more time, had supervisors who had concerns about their performance, continued, but still had a way to go before succeeding. "Yes, I Can Do It, But Do I Want To?" describes those who had considerable self-doubt, despite accolades from their supervisors. "Ready To Teach On My Own" describes those who experienced success and built self-confidence. "Mediating Stress" is a case illustration of a student teacher, Kelly Taylor, who reflected in an E-mail journal upon how she dealt with classroom stressors. All student and teacher names have been changed to ensure confidentiality. Kelly's account is powerful because it captures the evolving relationship between a challenging student and a caring student teacher—the trials, disappointments, perseverance, and hope.

Struggles Without Success: Not a Good Match

The following case illustration demonstrates the rising levels of stress that occur in the classroom when adults who are responsible for children, in this case student teachers, respond inappropriately. Janice Riley enrolled in a graduate program thinking that teaching was the field for her. After completing her Bachelor of Arts degree, she had tried a series of other jobs, but was disappointed with them. Early in the semester, Mrs. Barnes, her cooperating teacher, and I became concerned when the 2nd-grade children who otherwise had been cooperative began exhibiting inappropriate behavior under Janice's supervision. In addition, we found that Janice had not followed through with important behind-the-scene preparations, such as creating thorough lesson plans. Furthermore, Janice had missed several teaching days, but did not provide Mrs. Barnes with the lesson materials she had prepared. Mrs. Barnes often had to interject comments in Janice's lessons to keep students focused on the objective and ensure that learning was taking place. As the weeks unfolded, Mrs. Barnes and I kept anecdotal records and identified the following problem areas: Janice's expectations were confusing to students, she did not check for student understanding, and the lesson pace was often too slow. It was obvious that Janice was unaware of her many inappropriate classroom management strategies; when constructive criticism was offered, Janice would react by being argumentative and/or self-deprecating. It was becoming obvious that Janice was not developing as an authority figure; she did not inspire confidence in the children. She did not demonstrate an ability to adequately take care of their needs and help them grow socially and intellectually. As is often the case, Janice's classroom management difficulties were linked in some way to inadequate instructional preparation or implementation.

The following anecdotal records kept by Mrs. Barnes, with my interpretations in brackets, clarify the nature of Janice's difficulties.

> [Inability to create a climate of security and trust]:
>
> In the midst of a "real" fire drill a professional does not look bewildered and alarmed and say in front of the children, "I mean . . . what is going on here?!" I told Janice to turn away from the building and look at the children in a calm, reassuring manner. If you are to be responsible for an entire class during a crisis, it is vital to maintain your own composure.
>
> During a math lesson, [one] child had a nosebleed. I did what every veteran teacher would do—pinched with one hand and kept teaching. Janice looked very upset at the sight and kept walking over towards the child and me and said, "Is he going to be all right?!" Since I hadn't skipped a beat in my lesson she should have sensed that all was under control; [she] should have focused her attention on the other students, away from the crisis as in the fire drill episode.

She often shows the children how flustered she is through body language, facial expression, and voice tone, rather than maintaining a calm "I can fix it" attitude.

Janice was asked to take the children to the bus. We have a very set routine [in which] students must stop at the end of the sidewalk and wait until the teacher sees that it is safe and clear [to cross]. They may go when teachers say to walk. Janice did not follow this procedure and two children ran into a child in a wheelchair.

[Lack of Instructional Competence]:

Quite frequently Janice made punctuation errors on the chalkboard or overhead projector. Often the children corrected her before I could discreetly help her spot her mistakes. Janice knows she is weak in English grammar and spelling and [so she] carries a pocket guide with her. I know no one is perfect and sometimes nervousness will cause you to make a few careless mistakes, but a college graduate implies a certain mastery of elementary English grammar, [one] who should not require a pocket guide. Of course, that is just my opinion.

When discussing *The Giant Beet*, Janice told the children to read the next page to find out what the Queen does with the beet. On those pages the Queen does nothing with the beet. I asked [Janice] if she had read the story before the lesson and she said, "Yes, I read all the stories during spring break." Reading a story one time, a week ago, is not enough preparation to guide students through key story elements. I had told Janice several times before that she could use the questions and reading for purpose set which is clearly marked out in the teacher's guide. This story is ripe for character analysis and motives. When it was evident Janice wasn't even touching these points, I joined the discussion. The main focus of the story was the contrast of the poor but generous woman and her greedy, rich brother. In short, Janice had not been thoroughly prepared to do more than a superficial page turning through the story.

[Children's Reactions to Janice]:

Janice reported to me that one of the boys in the class said he couldn't figure her out—she didn't act like a grown-up but she looked too old to be a child. What was she?

[Sometimes, the children are encouraged to offer comments about their student teacher.] On a student survey most [of the] children said that their student teacher thinks they can behave; yet almost every child said she was angry sometimes or a lot. When asked what bothered them, most children responded "when she was mad, angry, or fussing at someone." I had often counseled Janice to "catch them being good" and emphasize the positive. And if they "got to her," not to let it show, not to [belabor] the point, but treat situations quickly and matter-of-factly. This lack of a positive attitude often created a depressing, no-win situation with the children. Unfortunately, the children were disrespectful to her when I was not within earshot. One child argued and yelled at [Janice] and she kept arguing with him; this child had no history of being disrespectful, and for me had usually been cheerfully cooperative.

Mrs. Barnes's poignant comments reflect her dedication to, and awareness of, the 2nd-graders' needs, as well as an astute evaluation of Janice's shortcomings. "Shortcomings" may sound harsh, but is unfortunately warranted in this case. If Janice had accepted more responsibility for her difficulties rather than casting blame on the children, our assessments would have been tempered with the sentiment that teaching just was not a good match for Janice's capabilities. Instead, Janice projected the attitude that she would somehow make it through because, after all, how difficult could it be to teach

2nd-graders? What Janice failed to see was her own need to grow before she would be ready to provide a stimulating and secure environment in which children could learn about themselves, others, and the world around them.

On the Student Teacher Observation Form that I completed for Janice's third observation, I recorded a statement made by Janice when she was in the middle of teaching a lesson. After a period of considerable disruption and lack of attentiveness that Janice had been unable to redirect positively, she looked across the room at me and said in a voice that all the children could hear, "See what I mean; I have no control." This statement not only reveals a great deal about Janice's lack of self-confidence, but also demonstrates a complete disregard for the children. Did she not have enough appreciation for their character and development to realize that they could not be expected to respect her if she had no respect for herself? Children need to feel that the adults in the classroom are there to teach and protect them, not the other way around. When children are not allowed to be children, stress is sure to follow.

In the end, Janice was counseled out of student teaching, a necessary requirement for licensure. Therefore, she was not granted a teaching certificate.

If At First You Don't Succeed

Occasionally, stress becomes evident when there is not a good fit between a student teacher and children. This was the case for Roger Bentley. In contrast to Janice, who blamed others for her lack of success, Roger demonstrated a strong commitment to be effective. Wanting to do well, however, did not ensure success with 6th-graders during his semester of student teaching. In the beginning, Roger's cooperating teacher, Ms. Creighton, and I offered support and encouragement. During feedback sessions, we found Roger to be receptive and able to suggest ways to improve his efforts working with uncooperative students. But soon we noticed that while Roger was quite long-winded regarding learning theories and teaching strategies during our one-to-one feedback conferences, pandemonium was becoming the norm in the classroom.

Ms. Creighton and I began to see patterns in Roger's teaching methodology that were causing students to react in understandably negative ways. Roger was talking too much, the lesson pace was too slow, he was listening only superficially, he was trying to be "with it" but not succeeding, and he was not giving adequate support or connection to student responses.

The first time I observed Roger, his lesson included reading an excerpt from a story about a boy, his dog who had to have chemotherapy, and the vet who was caring for the dog. Roger read the excerpt with good expression and I found myself holding back tears. I was very touched and glad to see that Roger's selection would generate such great discussion. But the discussion never happened. Instead, the opportunity for exploring emotions and sharing experiences with pets was lost when Roger referred students to a writing prompt, asking them to write in their journals. While his assignment was a good one, the students never had an opportunity to share their journal entries or discuss the story.

I felt a dismissive cloud hang in the air. Sensing what the students must have felt, I became increasingly concerned that Roger did not know how to relate to 6th-graders. He was not making connections between the subject matter and the students, something the students were quite eager and willing to do. We discussed this in the feedback conference and Roger was quite open to the possibility of having such a discussion. He added that he could have shared a personal experience with a cat that had died unexpectedly. This was only the first observation, and so I remained hopeful. It soon became evident, however, that Roger had difficulty responding to those teaching moments, either spontaneously or when planned into the lesson. A serious problem with student rapport is indicated by Ms. Creighton's comments on Roger's evaluation form:

> Roger has had tremendous difficulty in creating a rapport with students. Through his mannerisms he has lost the respect of many students, which has ultimately led to behavior management problems. Roger has difficulty responding to non-verbal cues from students [when] they may be bored or inattentive. For example, on more than one occasion, I have asked Roger to shorten his "while you waits" [these are attention-getting activities used to begin a lesson, typically lasting no more than 10-15 minute]. Roger's [activities] have lasted upwards of 35 minutes. I've seen the students lose their focus and become inattentive. In the area of sensitivity, I have witnessed Roger cut off students mid-sentence, dismiss their suggestions, and embarrass them in front of their peers.

Roger's tendency to "need an audience" carried over into his interactions with adults. During our post-observation sessions, Roger could enumerate, at length, ways that the lesson could be changed. Comments from Ms. Creighton suggest that Roger also needed to make some changes in his socializing habits in the workplace.

> It appears to me that Roger has not efficiently used his time inside or outside of the classroom. He spent the majority of his planning time as well as time after school hanging around in other teachers' classrooms seeking social interactions and opportunities to "vent" his day. It would seem that he should be too busy grading and planning to have this much time to socialize. Relating back to professional demeanor, several professionals have expressed concerns to me about needing [their own] personal time and I've shared that with Roger.

It is quite unusual to receive such feedback about a student teacher. For the most part, student teachers, like most adults, pick up on subtleties and know when it is appropriate to work and when to be sociable. But Roger was an extreme case. Once engaged verbally, he had difficulty disengaging. I found it necessary to institute a plan whereby he knew that our post-observation conferences were to last no longer than 30 minutes. (I had never had to set a time limit before.) I told Roger that he needed to address his ability to end the conference. It was his responsibility to watch the time and find a diplomatic way to stop when the 30 minutes had passed. He responded positively and was more effective during our next conference.

Because Roger was receptive to very direct feedback and was willing to change, his cooperating teacher and I believed that he could grow personally and professionally. We felt he was a long way from being effective with young adolescents, however. He just did not have the personality and self-confidence to be with students who were in transition from childhood to adolescence. Children at that age need guidance from adults, yet have strong ties to peers. Roger had difficulty identifying and relating to that developmental characteristic. Additional observations of Roger in the college classroom showed that he had difficulty relating to his own peers; he had trouble just fitting in with his cohorts, both men and women.

For a host of reasons, I recommended that he repeat student teaching in a 3rd-grade classroom, specifying personal and professional areas of needed growth. Although this was a great blow to Roger, he accepted the challenge. He met with his new cooperating teacher over the summer to familiarize himself with her goals, philosophy, and the 3rd-grade curriculum and get a head start on thoroughly planning and preparing for the assignment. In addition, the cooperating teacher had an opportunity to get acquainted with Roger's aspirations and become more fully informed of his experience with 6th-graders. I selected his second cooperating teacher, who had over 30 years of teaching experience, knowing that she would be compassionate with Roger, but unlikely to let an individual enter the teaching profession if there were any doubts about his competence in working with young people.

Having been given a second chance and greater clarity of expectations, Roger began the semester on a positive note. His planning and preparation had improved, thus increasing the effectiveness of his lessons and gaining him more positive feedback from the children. Still somewhat stiff in the beginning, Roger grew in confidence. As he saw the relationship between lesson design, listening to children, and making adjustments based on their feedback, he started to relax. These dynamic forces are enough of a challenge without worrying about how to be considered a "cool" teacher, something that had been an additional source of frustration during Roger's work with 6th-graders. On his final evaluation, I communicated that, based on what I had observed, Roger was better suited for elementary teaching at this stage in his career.

Several lessons may be learned from Roger's experience. As a student teacher, it is important to think of oneself as someone who is growing. The student teaching semester is an opportunity to develop in the role of a teacher, but it is also an opportunity to learn about oneself. Reflecting upon the age level or levels one is most comfortable working with is a very significant part of learning about career options and deciding how to interview for a job. Some student teachers are quite comfortable with children in many stages of development, whereas others have strong feelings about limiting their options to a span of one or two years. The student teaching experience is a two-way process, as we have seen from aspects of Janice's and Roger's stories. Children know when someone is succeeding, and their responses should be respected. I am no longer surprised when children as young as 7 find a way to whisper to me during an observation that Ms. Jones or Mr. Brown "is doing a good job."

Feelings of mutual respect create a positive atmosphere in the classroom. When respect and understanding are not present, however, both adults and children will feel stress. One should not throw in the towel when this occurs; after all, student teachers are still students and deserve the respect and understanding that will help them grow. Sometimes, a placement in a certain setting presents too many challenges to handle at one time. Professional growth cannot be rushed. Working with children brings many rewards, but only if the children are certain that you care about their social, emotional, and intellectual needs and are able to translate that dedication into practice.

Yes, I Can Do It, But Do I Want To?

Occasionally, certain classrooms develop a reputation for having several or even many children with emotional problems. As a college supervisor, it is not my place to question the wisdom of clustering such children into one classroom. Sometimes, the casual explanation is that the teacher has been successful working with children who have emotional needs. While this may be the case, I *am* surprised when a student teacher's first assignment is in such a classroom. As student teaching placements have become more problematic, due to the increasing number of student teachers and the limited number of sites close to college campus, these kinds of placements have become more common than in the past. We might think of these conditions as a recipe for stress.

Ann Marie's student teaching placement was in just such a classroom. Her cooperating teacher, Mrs. Stone, always brought to my mind lines from "The New Colossus," Emma Lazarus's poem that is inscribed on the Statue of Liberty: "Give me your tired, your poor, your huddled masses yearning to be free. . . ." Mrs. Stone had that aura about her! A woman with enthusiasm and a chatty and positive demeanor, it seemed that nothing could detract from her optimism. She was highly verbal and mediated the classroom disruptions by talking more than the students did; for this group of students, that strategy seemed to keep them engaged in various forms of the learning process. Ann Marie was very strong academically, poised, assertive yet reserved at the same time, creative, and very responsible and thorough in her work. On a Student Teacher Personal Data Sheet, Ann Marie described herself as "interested in the environment and nature, proficient in French, musically inclined, interested in arts and crafts (painting, ceramics, knitting)."

Both Mrs. Stone and I felt that Ann Marie was successful during her student teaching and that she would make a wonderful teacher. The following comments on Mrs. Stone's final evaluation form reflect this sentiment:

> Based on my work with and observation of Ann Marie throughout her student teaching assignment I consider her performance to be outstanding. She consistently demonstrated the personal and professional qualities that are reflected in a successful classroom teacher. Of particular note are her cooperativeness, her flexibility in coping with a variety of classroom situations, and the initiative with which she approached her classroom responsibilities. Ann Marie quickly developed rapport with the students. Additionally, she demonstrated a sensitivity and understanding for working with all [of the] children in the classroom. She demonstrated a high level of competence for instructional planning, student assessment, subject matter knowledge, and instructional delivery. Regarding student management, Ann Marie stepped into a challenging classroom situation that included several special needs students, and performed remarkably well. The children responded well to her warmth and positive demeanor. I am convinced that Ann Marie will have a very successful teaching career.

While Ann Marie was happy to receive high recommendations from both of us, I knew that she did not have a positive experience and that she concluded the program feeling very frustrated. Her high marks did not tell the entire story; she was having doubts about her ability and willingness to pursue a teaching career. She raised such questions as, "Why would I want to be in a situation where I had spent hours designing creative and motivational lessons, only to spend 60 percent of the lesson teaching students manners that they should already have?" Or, "It's not in my nature to punish; most of the children do respond, but then there is a handful of children who ruin it for the others. I don't want to be the kind of person they seem to want me to be, which is giving out negative consequences. It detracts from the positive learning opportunities that the others are experiencing. It's not fair to them or to me!"

In a situation in which children with emotional problems have been clustered together, the potential for stress, both for the teacher and for all the students, is exceedingly high. From the teacher's point of view, he or she is responsible for a classroom that has more than its share of stress factors. While the individual teacher may be effective, a great deal of dependency builds up around this teacher. The class may be quite vulnerable when the regular teacher is out; when they go to other teachers (for art, music, technology, or physical education); or when a student teacher has full responsibility while the teacher is out of the room. Student teachers like Ann Marie hear experienced teachers lament the increase in the number of children under stress; it is important to stop and listen to the questions raised by the student teachers. Rather than suggest a few behavioral strategies, it makes sense to question educators' motives for encouraging education students to stick with pursuing the field if they truly are unhappy. In addition, it behooves educators to listen to the experiences of student teachers, because they may offer fresh ideas and insights.

Even with all her doubts and questions, Ann Marie did go into the teaching profession. During her first year as a kindergarten teacher, she had a wonderful time and found the parents and children to be a delight to know and teach. She was able to put her self-doubts behind her and grow in new ways. Unfortunately, her second and third years of teaching were not as rewarding. Some of the disturbing situations that she had encountered during student teaching recurred and she found the faculty lounge politics to be a drain on her energy. Ann Marie decided to take a break from teaching. Since then, she has written a children's book, opened an art gallery in partnership with a friend (where she also shows her own paintings), and is currently staying home to raise her two young daughters. I like to introduce Ann Marie as a model to my students who are preparing to teach. Ann Marie is talented, dedicated to children, and thoughtful about how her own personal and professional growth can influence others. She knew instinctively that to be effective, one has to be growing and happy both in and out of the classroom.

Ready To Teach on My Own

Of the hundreds of student teachers I have worked with, over 90 percent completed their experience and embarked upon a teaching career. It is important to put the overall student teaching experience in perspective, since most of the students are successful during their internship. The three following stories represent many notable qualities observed in student teachers. While stress factors were evident in the classrooms throughout their student teaching experience, the students managed to mediate situations smoothly. In their comments, one can discern a receptivity not only to individual students, but also to looking at the larger picture of how learning is taking place in the classroom; a willingness to reflect upon classroom situations and note both positive areas and areas needing improvement; an intellectual curiosity whereby they apply theories and philosophies of learning; and a sense of excitement and enthusiasm about children's learning and about the role they have played in facilitating that learning.

During the first five weeks of student teaching, the students I have worked with videotape themselves and self-evaluate their lessons. They are given several questions to address, such as whether or not objectives were met, if the lesson provided a sufficient challenge, what their motivational approaches were, and what their overall reactions are. The self-evaluations that follow reveal the ways student teachers constructively critique their teaching experiences. As most supervisors would agree, a novice who can balance the positive and constructive aspects of self-evaluation is more inclined to grow professionally. The novices who see their lessons in extremes—as close to perfection or only in negative terms—are less inclined to develop.

Katrina Mendez, Grade One Student Teacher

"During the lesson on gorillas, our class reviewed previously learned facts and read a portion of the *Gorilla Zoobook* as well as excerpts from *Wild Animals* by David Alderton. Throughout the reading, we frequently stopped to define or discuss difficult or key words, answer questions, or share our comments. The students then created gorilla murals that demonstrated their knowledge of gorilla behavior, habitat, and adaptations. Very little extrinsic motivation was necessary for this lesson. The students seem to love studying about the animals and reading zoo books and they retain an amazing amount of information. I did offer as extrinsic motivation the suggestion that in order to work on a special project (the murals), we really needed to learn more about gorillas. I did not overemphasize this goal because previous experience has shown me that the children will often become too curious, anxious, . . . [and therefore won't] . . . listen to the lesson.

I believe that this lesson was at the appropriate level of challenge and that the lesson's objectives were met. The students have proven frequently that they are eager and capable of comprehending information of this type. They were not required to listen quietly for an extended period, and after reading, they were able to be creative and use their knowledge in one of their favorite ways. The lesson closed with each of the groups presenting and explaining their murals. Their explanations and drawings proved that the lesson's objective of describing habits, habitats, and adaptations of gorillas had been met. There were lots of jungles with heavy foliage as well as many adult gorillas knucklewalking, chest beating, and eating as young gorillas played in the trees.

Overall, I feel that this lesson was successful. I did feel that I seemed distracted, and perhaps I need to work on focusing on the children despite distractions. I learned a lesson on grouping and plan to make this less complicated and disruptive in future attempts. Once the groups were settled, they were very productive despite the beginning chaos! On a scale of 0 to 10, I would rate this lesson as a strong 7."

Katrina reveals how encouraged she finds the children's natural desire to learn, given subject matter that is appropriate for their age. She is sensitive to their excitement about working on the mural and knows that they should not be expected to sit and listen to her for a lengthy period of time. Yet, she also knows that unless she teaches them something about gorillas, their murals will be limited. Therefore, she has captured the appropriate balance between challenging her students intellectually and engaging them in the creative process. The two are not mutually exclusive activities, but rather go hand in hand. In addition, she notes that she appeared distracted. Katrina realized from viewing the tape that the children were very much involved in the lesson and that perhaps her distraction was unnecessary. The feedback provided by the videotape affirmed Katrina's effectiveness, enabling her to relax more about her performance, become more self-confident, and concentrate on the children's needs.

Grace Fields, Grade Two Student Teacher

"Yes, I felt I met the purpose and objectives, which were to assess and provide multiplication readiness, in that the student would be able to name the numeral that results from joining equivalent sets. I think this because of the participation I got in the class and the performance of the students on the worksheets. The few errors that occurred were more often counting errors than concept errors.

Yes, I think it was an appropriate challenge for the majority of the students. Even those few [who] professed to knowing their times tables seemed to get something from the conceptual part of the lesson. About half the class already knew that 1 x # = #, but, again, they learned why that was so."

"Motivational technique—the major one that I used in this lesson was involvement. Each student had his/her own beans/shells to work out the problem.

Visuals—overhead to show bean groupings; overhead of the first worksheet to model. Manipulatives=counters (beans or shells). I think both were effective, in that the counters showed, concretely, the concept of multiplication. The overhead allowed the students to see me model exactly what I wanted them to do.

Overall reactions—I thought this was an excellent tool to show not only what was being done incorrectly, but also to point out what was done well. This was a surprise to me since I had thought that my nervousness [at being videotaped] and sometimes [my] frustration was apparent, but found that it really wasn't. I think I need to find a better way to pass things out (e.g., counters, worksheets) and to use the overhead. Both of these activities enhanced the lesson, but also disrupted it. I also needed to have an option of other problems for [those] students . . . who quickly caught on and then began to fidget. Overall, though, I was much more pleased with both the lesson and the videotape than I thought I'd be."

Grace also clearly communicates her enthusiasm about the students' learning. She is obviously striving toward helping the students improve their conceptual understanding of equivalent sets. She wanted her students to be able to explain why the sets were equivalent so as to demonstrate whether or not they had grasped the concept. With proper guidance, the children met the challenge of Grace's high expectations. While Grace acknowledged that her objectives were met, she identified other issues she needed to address (e.g., ways to extend the lesson for those students who caught on quickly). The teaching-learning process is truly a two-way street! Grace picked up on the subtle homework assignment that the students created for her—how to address the boredom that can result in fidgeting. As Katrina had been, Grace was relieved to find that her feelings of nervousness had not been apparent and seemed unwarranted. Seeing her own effectiveness captured on tape bolstered Grace's self-confidence.

Carl Johnson, Grade Five Student Teacher

"On Wednesday, I taught a lesson on median in math class. This was the last formal lesson I would teach in cluster two of the math. On the day the video was taken, [my cooperating teacher] attended a special presentation at William and Mary. This was exciting because I would see if the classroom control was because they knew that [she] was in the room or was it something I did. I found out that it was as orderly as when [she] was in the room.

The objectives of the lesson were to (1) find the median of a set of numbers and (2) distinguish the median from the mean. They learned about mean the day before. A majority of the class had a good grasp of the concept based on how they did on the homework. A few during class skipped the first step of putting the numbers in order but after I reminded them they did OK.

The lesson started after a grueling quiz on long division. They understand long division, but it's so easy to make a mistake and it takes so long. So the motivational technique was [to move] on to something easier and then I got them thinking with a little brain teaser, "Why did I pick number seven?" This was a lesson challenging to them because it was new. Since they had heard of average before, which was related, it wasn't too hard. Because this lesson was taught after the quiz it was a short lesson so I didn't have many manipulatives, but I did use a visual of colored blocks on the overhead. The lesson closed with my asking them what they learned and it was clear it was the end of the day when I got answers like "nothin'." But I think it was important that they got a chance to tell me in their words what they learned instead of me telling them again.

My overall reaction is that the lesson went pretty well. It was a shorter lesson so I couldn't develop the lesson as much as I would have liked. Also it wasn't as much fun as some of the other lessons and I didn't tell them why medians are important. I did like the classroom control and I did like the guided practice and the closure."

Carl, like the other two student teachers, creates a healthy balance when analyzing his effectiveness in the lesson. One cannot be a perfectionist when working with children—or people of any age, for that matter! Burnout comes quickly to those who expect every lesson to be perfect. It was refreshing to see the reassurance he felt in the absence of his teacher and also to see how secure he was in admitting that some of the students said they learned "nothin'." Coming from 5th-graders, this statement should not be taken at face value, something Carl learned from experience. Carl, Katrina, and Grace are on their way, knowing they have a lot to learn, but full of confidence as a result of the tutelage and support they received from experienced cooperating teachers.

Each of these examples might give the impression that the student teachers faced no major stress factors. First-graders being "anxious" about the mural, bright 2nd-graders beginning to "fidget," and 5th-graders saying they learned "nothin'" hardly reflect high stress levels for student teachers. Were the situations relatively stress-free because each of the student teachers happened to have a class with a low percentage of children with significant emotional problems? Or, did things proceed smoothly because the student teachers were receptive to their students' developmental needs? Was the success a result of the lessons being motivational? Countless factors coming together contribute to establishing a positive classroom ethos, wherein stressors and potentially stressful interactions are mediated in a supportive manner.

It is quite possible that some of the children in these classrooms were experiencing various forms of turmoil—loss, family discord, discrimination, academic frustration, and so on. This is the reality that teachers face when they teach. In ideal circumstances, these life stressors would be mediated by the teacher through effective planning, sensitivity to children, creativity, dedication, and a strong desire to help children grow intellectually, socially, and emotionally. Successful teachers and student teachers, along with parents and other caring adults, listen and address the needs of children who are experiencing stress. By opening other windows to the world, they provide hope and guide children toward a more positive course of action.

A Student Teacher's Personal Account of Mediating Stress

These student teaching case illustrations demonstrate the complexity of mediating stress when so many variables, including individual personalities, are unique to a specific context. What can we learn from someone who is asked to reflect upon the stress that he or she is mediating? When I found out that I would be writing a chapter that specifically examined how student teachers deal with children's stress factors in the classroom, I asked a student teacher who seemed quite sensitive to children's needs to keep an E-mail journal that would include her responses to my periodic questions. In the following passages, you will see how a child who poses difficulties in the classroom weighs heavily on Kelly's mind. Unlike the previous sections that characterized stress over the course of a 10-week experience, this section captures the intensity of day-to-day interactions.

October Question: Are there students who seem to be creating difficulties for you when you teach or interact in the classroom? If so, please describe them (or one of them) and explain how you are responding.
Kelly's Response: Jen fairly constantly proves difficult to work with and interact with. She demands attention constantly, and when she receives it (often through being reminded to behave, etc.), she seems to be receptive, replying "yes" to every question (e.g., "Do you understand?" "Will you change your behavior?"), yet moments later reverting to misbehavior. She demands attention through misbehaving, not paying attention, blurting things out at inappropriate times, singing in the trailer's bathroom, etc. She has been a trial for me, in that I don't want to focus my attention on her and give her exactly what she wants, yet she creates such a disruption that she MUST be attended to!! Furthermore, it hurts to see her not achieve, and I would love to see a change in her behavior, and more importantly, her attitude (she certainly has an attitude that is not easy to work with!!). At the [outset], I allowed her behavior to get to me mentally and affect [me the rest] of the day, but when I realized . . . [that] the majority of the class [was] extremely attentive, interested, and hard-working, I decided not to allow her to get under my skin. I came to this through speaking with my cooperating teacher at length about the situation, and she feels equally frustrated. One problem is that Jen sits right in front of our desks (we're at the back of the room), and thus we notice her more often and tend to correct any misbehavior. We plan to move her, although she needs to be somewhat isolated, because she pulls virtually all but the extremely diligent and confident students into misbehaving!! [Moving her to another desk] will keep us from focusing our attention too much on her. Additionally, we have talked to her numerous times, trying to encourage, praise, and express our high expectations . . ., but unfortunately these [efforts] all [met] with little success. My teacher doesn't want us to spend too much time with [Jen] because that's simply giving her what she wants and not expecting the same of her as [we do from] the rest of the students (i.e., we won't constantly refocus her). I seek out her good actions and praise her, but am trying to devote as much attention to all the other students as well. Finally, she may be paired with another teacher (her teacher from last year) in a "Sunshine program," which is a kind of partnership between a teacher [who is not the] child's [regular] teacher and a student causing disruption. [Children in this program] are account-

able to [these teachers] and have their own rewards and consequences outside of the class. We'll see how this goes. I think all will turn out fine, and I'm learning a lot through this experience with Jen. I can only do so much, and must devote most of my energy to helping the majority of students accomplish all they can.

November Question: What do you know about Jen's family and relationships with peers?
Kelly's Response: Here's all I could come up with for Jen's background (I'll be attending a conference with her mom soon, so will let you know more then). Jen lives with her mother and two sisters; she's the middle child. As far as we know, there is no father in the picture. Jen tells us that her mom says that she's basically the best of the bunch. She lives in a fairly poor area, from what we can tell. That's all I know of her home life as of now.

She's African American and spends [most of her] time [at school] with other African Americans. . . . She doesn't get along well with many [children] in our class—she quickly "catches an attitude" with virtually anyone. Jen does get along well with the two gentlest children in our class, a boy and a girl. These two are . . . [among] the most cheerful and loving children I've ever seen! These two get along with Jen fine, and Jen almost takes a motherly approach towards them (playing with their hair, etc.). Although she may also have a crush on the boy!!

We have a newspaper guild that the children apply to, which meets before school two days a week, and my teacher and I decided [Jen] could join. We're hoping this positive academic and fun experience will motivate her behaviorally and academically. In order to [continue working on the] newspaper, [Jen's] behavior and work must be up to par. We'll see how that goes.

A few weeks later: . . . I wanted to update you on Jen. I said that I would get back to you after our conference, and [it's] telling [to me that] her mom never showed up, [even] after several phone calls from my teacher, and after confirming [that she would meet with us]. Unfortunately she was, I believe, the only parent who never met with my teacher and me. Her family does not have a phone, which contributes to the problem, naturally (messages are relayed through an uncle). Therefore there's not much more I can tell you in relation to her background. . . . I'm having a wonderful experience overall, and I think it's primarily because our classroom is well managed, which is more important than I'd ever imagined and plays a significant role in the comparatively low stress level I've felt these weeks.

Post-Student Teaching December Conference

Question: Bring me up-to-date about Jen. How are you feeling about Jen, now that you have completed the student teaching semester?
Kelly's Response: After parent conferences, [her mother] called to say she wanted to meet [with us,] but still didn't come. The teacher wonders if Jen is the age she says she is. She is starting to act like an adolescent, very interested in boys. She is at least 11 but might be 12 or 13. She seems very "surface"; it is hard to get to know her. She is very laissez-faire about everything and [often] says "I don't care." The semester became less stressful. We moved Jen away from the desk [in the back] and put the students into cooperative groups. We put her with two girls who were friendly and strong academically. She was distracting the girls [and so] we gave her consequences (e.g., her name on the board, 10 minutes off recess). I don't feel these are working as a deterrent.

I can honestly say that I don't feel I have connected with [Jen], whereas I feel I have connected with everyone else and I don't like what that might say about myself. My cooperating teacher said not to let one student give so much stress to me. But she is also concerned about losing this student because it seems that [Jen's attitude] is getting worse . . . [she doesn't care] about anything. It is a realistic thing for me to realize that I am not going to be able to touch everyone or be everyone's saving grace.

Question: Have there been phases of coming to accept not connecting with Jen?
Kelly's response: It has always been important to me to show that I really care about her and I have worked so hard to love her. . . . The question is, how do I show her love? When I think of the 3rd-grade teacher who had the most impact on my life, I think of the way that she loved every student. Though she tells me that she doesn't love every student—it's just that you see that she does. To everyone else it looks as if I did fine but I feel as if I didn't do as much as I could have. There would be moments or days where I would feel, "Wow, I am really caring about her!" And on other days, [I'd think] "Where is your compassion?"

You never see [Jen] reacting with any feeling. I've . . . thought, "Even if I did care about you, you don't really care." I can't let this drag me down. Giving her so much of my attention is not benefiting anyone. She may be toned down but maybe it is me also just letting her be that way. At the end of the semester, I wrote letters to everyone and to her I [wrote] that we had some ups and downs and that she needed to make some decisions about her life. I haven't been able to process all of this. I have such good memories about all the other students. When thinking about [Jen in particular], I don't think of the good times, I think of the frustrating times. I don't know why you can't see the emotions or the real side of her, it's as if you don't really know her. I am the opposite because I am so up front with my feelings [and] I am very open.

We can see that Kelly is a very caring, open, and compassionate student teacher, the kind of person who will create a warm classroom environment and one who will be dedicated to opening the minds of her students. Kelly also has revealed a glimpse of the stressful teacher-student relationship that exists when people do not feel connected in some emotional way, or in a way that is mutually supportive. Certainly, the emotional needs of teachers and students are different, and teacher-student relationships vary in their level of intensity. Kelly has illuminated the stress a teacher feels when trying to offset a student's apathy. It is difficult to second-guess what perspectives Jen would have about her relationships and classroom behaviors. We can only acknowledge that academic achievement was not a high priority in Jen's life as a 5th-grader. Depending on Jen's future choices, her attitude may or may not change.

Coping With Stress in the Classroom

It is appropriate to raise awareness among novice and experienced teachers of the emotional stress often associated with teaching and its lasting effects. From talking with colleagues, experienced teachers, current students, and former students who have pursued or left teaching, I am saddened to see the permanent emotional scars on those who have invested so much of themselves to children and their families. In class, during student reunions, or in casual conversations, teachers and former teachers find themselves in tears, unexpectedly unleashing emotions that have been suppressed because of the need to carry on with the next group of children under their care.

Not long ago, a retired teacher told me that people he had encountered kept remarking how he looked 10 years younger, now that he had retired! He said that as he had shed the daily stress and reflected upon the past, he was able to find the long-lost happy person who had been submerged by everyone else's problems. We need to re-examine the unrealistic expectations of teachers, held both by themselves and by others, that lead to untoward stress levels, job dissatisfaction, and burnout. While these examinations will inevitably lead to long-term goals and solutions, more tangible supports are available for the immediate future.

Grant and Grant (1982) provide educators and counselors the following suggestions for helping children gain the coping skills they need for survival:

- Learn to recognize the early signs of excessive stress. Productive stress management requires early identification.
- Be positive and remain calm in counseling anxious children. Children under stress often lack self-esteem.
- Be sensitive to individual and cultural differences. No two children can cope with anxiety in the same way.
- Pay attention to dramatic changes in behavior. Frequent absenteeism, a sudden drop in academic performance, an increased number of illnesses, and disruptive behavior may be indicators of a crisis.
- Help children understand that they are not alone. Reach out and be available to them.
- Encourage children to communicate what they feel. Group counseling, home visits, role-play games, and drawings may help establish a rapport.

For members of the helping profession, whether novices or veterans, the following suggestions also may be helpful. The ideas have emerged from observing experienced and novice teachers who have shared their passions and heartfelt emotions when they found themselves emotionally distraught by the stress levels in the classroom. These ideas also emerged from observing experienced and novice teachers mediate stress with grace and confidence as they assure students that difficult situations may be overcome. These teachers and student teachers seem to communicate the message that learning and growing are challenges that require caring and commitment. In cases where children have experienced severe stress, these professionals seem to recognize that the caring and commitment is crucial, even if it is not acknowledged.

- Your emotional involvement means that you are a caring, sensitive, person. These qualities are the ones that can help you become an effective teacher. If they vanish, it may be time to leave the teaching profession!
- Do not give up or feel defeated if the students under stress do not respond in the ways you expect. Students intuitively know when you have "written them off"; if you do so, they may feel that you are yet another adult who does not care about them. It may mean a great deal to them that you care, even if they do not change their behavior the way you would like.
- Inform and enlist the support of fellow teachers, administrators, counselors, school psychologists, social workers, and other helping professionals. Effective coping requires reaching out to others for help.
- Recognize when you need to step back from a situation. Are you all-consumed by the needs of one or two students? Perhaps you need to regain perspective by thinking of the needs of the other students for whom you are responsible. Is crisis management something that preoccupies you to the point that you cannot address your other job responsibilities?
- Teachers wear many hats: nurturer, facilitator, disseminator of knowledge, leader, guide, counselor, coach, entertainer, resource. Think about the metaphors that you use to describe the role that has drawn you to the teaching profession. Do the metaphors fit with the reality of the classroom environment? For example, think about Kelly's realization that she was not going to be everyone's "saving grace."

- Try to recognize that you cannot be all things to all people. It is sometimes difficult to realize that there is no guarantee that you will automatically like children, or that they will like you. Every child, like any adult, has a unique personality and a singular background, seldom totally compatible with yours. Most elementary teachers have a middle-class background, but must work with students across all class levels. This can create value conflicts.
- Be true to yourself. It is important to grow as you learn to mediate your own stress as well as children's stress. Recognize, however, when the stress you are experiencing has become self-destructive. You cannot be an effective teacher if the environment in which you work is not mutually supportive.

Lao-tzu's classic manual on the art of living, *Tao Te Ching* (Mitchell, 1988), offers peaceful thoughts for those who struggle with life's many challenges. I hope you will find comfort in his words as you mediate the stress in your life and the lives of others!

> Knowing others is intelligence;
> knowing yourself is true wisdom.
> Mastering others is strength;
> mastering yourself is true power.

References and Resources

Acheson, Keith A., & Gall, Meredith Damien. (1992). *Techniques in the clinical supervision of teachers: Preservice and inservice applications.* White Plains, NY: Longman.

Anderson, Debra J., Major, Robert L., & Mitchell, Richard R. (1992). *Teacher supervision that works: A guide for university supervisors.* New York: Praeger.

Brenner, Avis. (1997). *Helping children cope with stress.* San Francisco: Jossey-Bass.

Bullough, Robert V., Jr., & Gitlin, Andrew. (1995). *Becoming a student of teaching: Methodologies for exploring self and school context.* New York: Garland.

Bullough, Robert V., Jr., Knowles, J. Gary, & Crow, Nedra A. (1992). *Emerging as a teacher.* London: Routledge.

Deskin, Gerald, & Steckler, Greg. (1996). *When nothing makes sense: Disaster, crisis, and their effects on children.* Minneapolis, MN: Fairview Press.

Elkind, David. (1981). *The hurried child: Growing up too fast too soon.* Reading, MA: Addison-Wesley.

Garland, Colden, & Shippy, Virginia. (1995). *Guiding clinical experiences: Effective supervision in teacher education.* Norwood, NJ: Ablex.

George, Jean Craighead. (1959). *My side of the mountain.* New York: E. P. Dutton.

Grant, Arthur F., & Grant, Audrey. (1982). Children under stress: What every school counselor should know. *Journal of Non-White Concerns in Personnel and Guidance, 11*(1-2), 17-23.

Johnson, James Harmon. (1986). *Life events as stressors in childhood and adolescence.* Newbury Park, CA: Sage Publications.

Joseph, Pamela Bolotin, & Burnaford, Gail E. (Eds.). (1994). *Images of schoolteachers in twentieth-century America.* New York: St. Martin's Press.

McAllister, Elizabeth A., & Neubert, Gloria A. (1995). *New teachers helping new teachers: Preservice peer coaching.* Bloomington, IN: ERIC Clearinghouse on Reading, English, and Communication.

Mitchell, Stephen. (1988). *Tao te ching.* New York: HarperCollins.

Rand, Muriel K., & Shelton-Colangelo, Sharon. (1999). *Voices of student teachers: Cases from the field.* Upper Saddle River, NJ: Merrill.

Slick, Gloria Appelt. (1995). *Preparing new teachers: Operating successful field experience programs.* Thousand Oaks, CA: Corwin Press.

Varma, Ved. (Ed.). (1996). *Coping with children in stress.* Aldershot, England: Arena.

Wolff, Sula. (1981). *Children under stress* (2nd ed.). New York: Penguin Books.

Chapter 7
Experienced Teachers: Seeing Children Whole

Beverly Hardcastle Stanford

Gino arrived early, marched across the classroom, still empty of children, and headed straight for his desk in the back next to the windows. He threw his books on the desktop and collapsed in a heap over them. Head down, he began to wail and sob, pounding the desk with his fists.

I felt I knew Gino well and I liked him a lot. We had spent nearly a year together in the 6th-grade classroom, and I had become accustomed to his outbursts of emotion and had learned how to handle them. Joy, anger, frustration, enthusiasm—we all always knew how Gino felt about things. His father spoke with the same exuberance; and I enjoyed what I considered to be their Italian expressiveness. But this day's behavior was extreme, even for Gino.

I approached him quickly but spoke quietly, hoping to calm him. "Gino, what's wrong? What's the matter?"

Keeping his head down, he shouted something into his books. His poundings synchronized with the muffled words, and got louder with each repetition. Finally I understood them—"Gramps killed himself. Mom should have hid the gun better. She should have hid it better! Why didn't she hide it better?!"

More students arrived, but they huddled at the door. Their eyes questioned me. I signaled to them to wait in the hall. Then I sat next to Gino and we talked. I asked questions; he responded. I assured him that his mother was angry and sad, too. Talking seemed to calm him. Finally I asked if he was ready for the others to come in, and he nodded his assent.

Fortunately, the class had bonded as a group, and we had already talked about the death of another student's grandparent—Pam's grandmother. The natural kindness the children displayed toward Pam after that discussion had touched me. They used actions and gestures more than words, but Pam knew they cared. Those near her in class moved their desks closer to her. Two friends put their arms around her and walked with her in a tangle of arms and bobbing heads all the way to the lunchroom. Several begged her to sit by them at their table. Others verbally "fought" to have Pam on their team at recess. The children were similarly kind on Gino's day of tragedy. And Gino, like Pam, found that he was cared for and special in the eyes of his classmates.

Unfortunately, children are not protected from painful experiences like those of Gino and Pam, and they encounter stress in many other forms. What can teachers do to assist them? What can veteran teachers tell us about helping students with their stress? And how do they, as caretakers, avoid burning out themselves?

Experienced teachers who persevere in their teaching with enthusiasm, do so because of their love for students and ability to see them whole, in the context of their lives as well as the classroom. They remind us that in order to teach well, we need to reach the child first, and that takes understanding, especially when stress interferes. This chapter explores four areas of knowledge teachers can tap to help students with stress: 1) school from a child's perspective, 2) responses to children's stress, 3) caring and bully-free classrooms, and 4) ways to explore schoolchildren's stress. As a reminder that teachers need to attend to their own stress, the chapter concludes with lessons from positive veteran teachers who persevered in the profession while teaching in two of the nation's most stressful urban environments.

School From a Child's Perspective

Seeing through children's eyes helps us perceive ways we inadvertently contribute to their stress. The section that follows offers a glimpse, from a child's perspective, of the stressful aspects of being in school.

The Challenge to Adults

For adults attempting to understand children, the task of seeing the world through children's eyes is deceptively challenging and impossible to accomplish fully. Adults are at a loss for several reasons. First, our childhood memories become hazy as we grow older, and we cannot always remember in detail the experiences or feelings of our past. Second, we sometimes change our memories to increase our self-respect or justify our life decisions. As Brim (1992) explains, "We alter our memories to create coherent stories of our lives that explain our place in life and account for what happened to us" (p. 85). Third, we have changed cognitively and so review our memories from a different perspective, one informed by abstractions and schema unknown to us as children. And fourth, the world that children live in today is not the one that we lived in as children. Despite these barriers, attempting to view the child's perspective is a necessary first step if we are to better understand and guide children.

Once, as a 3rd-grade teacher, I stooped down to a student's eye level to say something to him. He, in turn, stooped down as well. There we were in the hallway, both stooping down and visiting! I laughed at the sight we made then, and value it now as a metaphor for our need to see things from a child's perspective and a reminder of the responsibility we have as a model for children so ready to imitate us.

The View From "Below." Children are "below" adults literally in stature, but also figuratively because they have less knowledge, information, skill, resources, and control. They are by nature dependent upon adults. Their vulnerability casts a shadow on childhood—comforting shade for some, darkness for others. They often feel misunderstood and fearful, and their incomplete cognitive development foreshortens their perspective.

As a consequence, teachers need to be sensitive to the power advantage they have in the classroom. They have control over the lives of children who are entrusted to them for six to seven hours a day, five days a week. Teachers determine when their students may have a drink of water, attend to their bathroom needs, move about the classroom, talk with their friends, ask questions, and participate in various academic activities. Through their own modeling, they have a significant impact on how the children regard others and themselves, and how they treat each other. Wise teachers use their power to lead well and to avert or correct hurtful behavior kindly and effectively.

The Stress of the Unknown. Even for adults, it takes courage to face the unknown. Children must face new experiences and situations on a regular basis. I remember one group of 8- and 9-year olds, strangers from different schools, who met with their parents, several doctoral students, and me to plan a pilot character camp—an academic camp emphasizing ethics and character development. Their restlessness and apprehension were obvious. We needed to select a character trait for the camp's focus and asked the group to participate in a value-ranking activity. Nearly all the children ranked "courage" as being most important. Interestingly, courage is missing from most published lists of virtues. Their parents, who placed "respect" and "responsibility" first on their lists, nodded when they learned their children's rankings. One remarked that her son was "off the walls with fear" before attending the gathering because he did not know anyone attending.

The same group discussed their fears regarding a future unknown—that of moving from elementary to middle school. When asked how they felt about going to middle school, a few children laughed nervously and said that older students told them they would be put into wastebaskets head first, have their pants pulled off, and even be beaten up. If such tales were true, they were frightening warnings of potential humiliation. If false, they were still stressful reminders of their vulnerability to "big kids."

Experienced teachers find ways of helping children bridge transitions from the known to the unknown: from home to kindergarten, elementary school to middle school, and middle school to high school. They know that helping them anticipate new experiences will reduce stress. Some kindergarten and 1st-grade teachers visit their students in their homes before the school year begins and thus orient their expectations. Some invite parents and children to school for a preview and provide older students with field trips to their new schools. Walking though a practice school day, without the presence of older students, can be comforting. Providing young students with "big brothers" and "big sisters" to look out for them can, ultimately, benefit both groups.

Children's Non-logical Thinking. Children think differently from adults and their reasoning is often illogical. "Children cannot understand many things that adults say because they lack the necessary intellectual structures to make sense of what they mean," David Wood writes (1998, p. 72). As Michael Salce, a school psychology student in one of my classes observed, it should not surprise us that young children who believe in Santa Claus and the Easter Bunny do not use the same logic adults do. Children do think differently, and adults who fail to shape their communications with them accordingly can cause unnecessary stress.

Literal Thinking. The literal nature of children's thinking sometimes leads to behaviors that cause them stress and baffle their teachers. For instance, they may misinterpret a teacher's directions. One child spent his entire journal writing time erasing all of his previous entries. When asked what he was doing, he replied that the teacher had said they should make their writing "perfect." He knew that his earlier entries were not "perfect," so he erased them all.

A tendency to think in absolutes often leads children to follow rules quite strictly, even when it is to their own disadvantage. For instance, they may follow the class rule of not leaving the classroom to go to the bathroom during certain specified times—reading groups, centers, math lessons—even when severely pressed by their physical needs. The result, of course, can be an embarrassing accident—wetting their pants in class, which is a stress rated very high on Yamamoto's children's stress scale (see Chapter 5).

Primitive Thinking. Children's primitive thinking about death also can be a major source of stress. I recall a 3rd-grade child, Mary, who was terrified as she began her first day of the school year. The moment she entered the classroom she clutched my arm with both hands and began crying and asking, "Am I going to die? Am I going to die? Is my mother going to die?" She somehow thought that being in school would cause her to die or her mother to die. My reassurances quieted her for brief periods, but then her tears and questions would begin again. I directed our activities that morning with one arm, while the other acted as a life raft of sorts for the genuinely distressed 8-year-old. Fortunately, her mother worked in the school cafeteria; when Mary saw her at lunch, her distress eased. The situation improved each day, as Mary seemed to realize that neither she nor her mother were going to die. Her former teachers, her mother, and I were never able to completely sort out her reasoning, but we did conclude that her fear was connected in some way to the death of her grandmother over the summer. Mary's terror was rooted in her inability to understand the concept of death.

Being Misunderstood. Children also can be distressed when they are misunderstood. For instance, the child who spits on his desk and rubs the moisture into the desktop to make it shine is likely to be admonished: "Don't do that!" When a child helps her friend get the answer to a math problem, she may be told she is cheating. In both instances, the children believed they were being helpful. Such simple misunderstandings can cause children to feel inadequate, embarrassed, ashamed, or guilty—all of which are stressful emotions.

Teachers' Awareness. Experienced teachers are typically aware of young children's tendency to think literally. Therefore, they may take time to check the children's understanding, asking them to repeat the directions or explain the rules. Experienced teachers also actively survey the whole class and are able to juggle attending to several matters at the same time. They have "with-it-ness," the term Kounin (1970) used to designate teachers' proverbial "eyes in the back of their head." As experienced, effective teachers "read" their classroom, they are able to spot signs of distress or confusion and respond before problems occur or stress intensifies.

Stressful Classroom Conditions

Experienced teachers are also mindful of the classroom conditions that cause stress for students and run counter to their natural needs. The findings of Philip Jackson reported in his now classic book, *Life in Classrooms* (1968), are just as pertinent today as when he first led a team of researchers in observing life in elementary classrooms.

Being in a Crowd. Jackson observed that "when twenty or thirty people must live and work together within a limited space for five or six hours a day," they are living in crowded conditions that produce the "unpublicized features of school life: delay, denial, interruption, and social distraction" (p. 17). All four features are sources of stress for anyone; for children, their impact is aggravated by their developmental stage.

Because of a classroom's crowded conditions, virtually anything that children do while there becomes public, Jackson noted. A student's slow progress through a test, the teacher's grades and written critical comments on papers, and students' errors while reading aloud are hard to hide from others who sit close by. Having our mistakes made public is stressful to most of us, regardless of our age.

The Stress of Delays. The present-centered nature of childhood makes having to wait particularly stressing. A colleague shared with me a humorous example of children's preference for the "here and now." When she was traveling with her family on an auto trip, she woke up from a nap in the back seat and asked, "Where are we?" and "What time is it?" Her 6-year-old daughter said, "Why Mommy, we're here! And it's now!" At school, waiting is a regular feature of the day. Children wait to line up to leave the room, wait for their turn to get a drink of water, wait to find out how they did on a test, wait to see if the teacher likes their story, and wait to tell the teacher about something important that happened at home.

Experienced teachers find ways to reduce waiting times and adapt classroom rituals and rules to accommodate individual needs. To provide children with the immediate feedback and extra attention they crave, teachers show children how to respond to each others' work, and they solicit support from parents, grandparents, community volunteers, older students, retired teachers, and interested staff.

Responses to Children's Stress

Stress caused by the challenges of childhood and pain of personal tragedies occurs in every classroom. Even in relatively small and homogenous classes, teachers will have students who misbehave, are troubled, or are involved in stressful situations. Fortunately—and perhaps because of the continual demand for it—good advice is available. The next section presents a range of problems, from minor misbehavior to potentially life-debilitating stressors, and offers the explanations and recommendations of five psychologists and educators.

Children's Misbehavior

Children frequently exhibit their stress through misbehavior. The works of Rudolf Dreikurs, a psychologist, and Selma Wassermann, an educator, offer helpful approaches for addressing both minor and serious misbehavior.

Mistaken Goals. Dreikurs's theory (1972) of mistaken goals can help teachers understand and respond to misbehavior that commonly occurs in classrooms. Dreikurs, an Adlerian psychologist, proposed that all behavior has a purpose, and that misbehavior is guided by four mistaken goals: attention, power, revenge, and helplessness. Dreikurs viewed the mistaken goals in a hierarchy, with attention being the mistaken goal of least concern and helplessness being the most serious.

Dreikurs believed that teachers can use their emotional reactions to a child's misbehavior as a gauge to determine which of the mistaken goals the child is pursuing. For example, if a teacher feels frustrated or annoyed, it is likely that the child is seeking attention. Examples of this common misbehavior are whining, hanging on their teachers, and deliberately falling off a chair or dropping books. When teachers feel threatened and wonder if they can handle a child's challenge to them, the child is probably seeking power. A child's refusal to complete an assignment or respond to a teacher's request, as well as other acts of defiance, are examples of this form of misbehavior. When a child's behavior causes a teacher to feel hurt or personally attacked, then the mistaken goal is likely to be revenge. Children telling teachers that they hate them, think they're unfair, or they're lazy are examples of such hurtful acts. Finally, when teachers feel helpless and wonder if they can ever help the child understand how to sit quietly, complete assignments, take turns, or learn a skill, the child's mistaken goal is probably helplessness.

Dreikurs not only offered a strategy for identifying mistaken goals, he also suggested solutions for each form of misbehavior, drawing on sound psychological principles. For the child seeking attention, teachers need to provide attention for good behavior and work to extinguish the bad behavior by ignoring it. Teachers can find ways to provide individual attention for such children by making special efforts themselves, by assigning classmates to be partners for them, or by seeking an adult or older student to act as a mentor. Teachers also can ensure that these particular children receive attention from the entire class by asking them to give class announcements, read the answer key for assignments, or conduct a mini lesson. Their unmet need may thus be addressed and its accompanying stress lessened.

When dealing with children who are pursuing the mistaken goal of power, teachers need to provide the power and not confront it head on. Dreikurs compared the situation to sailing in a storm—you are better off dropping your sail than making it more rigid. Instead, teachers can acknowledge the child's power: "I can't make you do your homework, that's your decision." Then, they can use natural or logical consequences: "However, if your homework is not completed, you will not be able to have recess with the others who have completed their work. But that's your decision." In doing so, the power of choosing is given to the child. The distinction between punishing a child by refusing to let a child have recess and letting the child choose not to earn recess is subtle but significant. The child's sense of power is increased, and the stress caused by being powerless is reduced.

Troubled Children. Wassermann (1992) offers a practical procedure that teachers can follow when encountering children in trouble. She points out that "it is helpful to remember that children's behavior is symptomatic. They don't do what they do just to annoy teachers" (p. 232). She recommends that teachers examine their distressed students' troubling behavior objectively, avoiding making assumptions about their students such as they don't care, are lazy, hate school, or have bad parents. Once they describe the behavior objectively, they should investigate further, exploring data sources such as "the child, school records, previous teachers, parents, siblings and others who may shed light on the nature of the trouble and its persistence" (Wassermann, 1992, p. 232). When enough data are collected to make a conjecture about the cause of the problem, Wassermann directs teachers to write a short working hypothesis—25 words or less—about the cause of the problem. Her illustration is helpful: "Jessemine is exhibiting highly withdrawn behavior. She seems extremely fearful. Data from home suggest an emotionally abusive mother whose demands on the child appear excessive" (Wassermann, 1992, p. 233). At this point, Wassermann encourages teachers to imagine themselves in the child's position and to consider how it would feel to be that child. She observes that developing such empathy can reduce teachers' inclinations to personalize the troubling behavior or assign unwarranted motivations to students.

Teachers also should acknowledge their reactions by writing in journals and visiting with colleagues. "Ventilating and owning feelings are a healthy way to discharge them and gain perspectives," Wassermann explains (1992, p. 233).

Teachers are then to develop a teaching plan, drawing on various resources—textbooks, school counselors, and consultants. They should monitor the plan's effectiveness by keeping a daily record of their own and their students' behaviors. Wassermann's final tip is to be patient: "It is unlikely, no matter how good your teaching plan, that you can remedy the troubles in a short treatment period" (1992, p. 233).

Stressful Situations

Classifying stress situations is a helpful way to begin the process of assisting stressed students. David Elkind (1998) categorizes these situations into three major types. Type A stress situations are those in which "the potential stress is both foreseeable and avoidable" (p. 197), like riding on a frightening roller coaster, going away to camp, and engaging with peers in risky mischief—name calling, fighting, vandalizing, being gang "wannabees," and experimenting with drugs. Teachers and parents can help children with Type A stress conditions by guiding them in making good decisions and in anticipating the consequences of participating in the avoidable situation. Role plays, educational drama, and conflict resolution exercises are several ways that teachers can give children opportunities to rehearse how they will deal with anxiety-causing situations in a safe and instructive environment.

Type B stress situations entail "those demands that are neither foreseeable nor avoidable" (1998, p. 198). Examples include accidents of man and nature, street and home violence, illnesses, parents' divorce, and a death in the family. Perhaps because young children have so few options in life, they seem to suffer from Type B stress disproportionately. I think of Gino and his grandfather's suicide. I also remember Mandy, a 7-year-old, large and mature for her age, who was put in charge of watching her little brother. One day, when she turned to pick up some toys she dropped, her brother ran into the street and was killed. Mandy had trouble concentrating in the 3rd-grade class the following fall, and she disliked it when her classmates asked her to be in charge in their play at recess.

Children who suffer the consequences of their parents' problems also experience this category of stress. I recall the 3rd-grade boy who kept a swimsuit glamour photo of his mother on his desktop all spring. It was his only tangible reminder of the woman who had walked out of his home and life. One of his classmates also felt the stress of abandonment. This boy told me every Friday that his father would come to see him during the weekend; each Monday, he would return to school disappointed and disheartened. And I remember the 5th-grader whose angry explosion in class was caused by his big sister's ultimatum that he decide, that very day, whether he would go out of state with her to live with their father or remain without her in town with their mother.

Children in abusive families also experience unforeseeable and unavoidable stress. Johnnie, a former student in my 6th-grade class, is an example. His urinary problems and below-average growth were attributed to his determination to stay awake at night and thus avoid being abused, a fate his siblings had not escaped. Charming and bright, Johnnie won the hearts of his classmates and me in the few months he spent with us before his family moved on once more, staying one step ahead of child protection services.

Clearly, these Type B stress conditions are the most serious and potentially damaging forms of stress. Experienced teachers are alert to signs of abuse—children's unexplained bruises, especially on their face; camouflaging clothing, such as long sleeves on hot days; precocious sexual play and talk; stained or bloody underwear; frequent fatigue; and aberrant behavior (i.e., extreme aggressiveness or passivity, intolerance to being touched, and stealing food). Attentive teachers report signs of abuse and partner with school psychologists and counselors on behalf of their students. They are sensitive to signs of problems revealed in young children's creative play, and they find appropriate literature to help older students. Most important, their care and availability enable them to be islands of safety and assistance for children tossed by life's rough seas.

Elkind (1998) describes Type C stress situations as "foreseeable yet not avoidable" (p. 200). Examples of Type C stressors for children would be vaccinations, getting a tooth pulled out at the dentist's, giving a speech or taking a test at school, and having to undergo surgery. Sometimes, the anticipation of such events can be more painful than the stressor itself, Elkind observes. Interestingly, dealing directly with the anticipation is one way to reduce the impact of these stressors. For instance, some hospitals have found that children's stress is reduced if a hospital employee or volunteer walks them through the operation experience ahead of time, taking them place to place and explaining what will happen at each point. A student in one of my classes played such a role, dressed as "The Blue Kangaroo," in a children's hospital in Austin, Texas. She enjoyed these experiences and was convinced that her young charges were less fearful after their rehearsals with her. Teachers can prepare children for anticipated stressful school experiences as well—giving children practice tests, exposing them to scantrons and test booklets in non-test situations, and having them practice their speeches in small groups.

Creative Outlets for Children's Stress

Art, music, drama, movement, and free play can act as creative outlets for children's stress. Sylvia Ashton-Warner (1963), whose reflections on teaching Maori children in New Zealand drew international attention, explained that creativity can release children's warlike tendency for destructiveness:

> So often I have seen the destructive vent, beneath an onslaught of creativity, dry up under my eyes. Especially with the warlike Maori five-year-olds who pass through my hands in hundreds, arriving with no other thought in their heads other than to take, break, fight and be first. . . . Yet all this can be expelled through the creative vent, and the more violent the boy the more I see that he creates . . . I put clay in his hands, or chalk. He can create bombs if he likes or draw my house in flame, but it is the creative vent that is widening all the time and the destructive one atrophying, however much it may look to the contrary. (p. 83).

In the mornings, Ashton-Warner played classical music—Beethoven, Chopin, Brahms, Grieg, and Tchaikovsky—and allowed the children to move and dance freely. Valuing the medium of dancing, she noted that "Plato said it was the one complete expression involving the faculties on all levels, spiritual, intellectual and physical" (1963, p. 80). She used dancing for children's creative output, but also "to break any strain of work during the day" (1963, p. 80).

Similarly, Vivian Paley uses creative play, storytelling, and drama to enable children to express and explore their feelings. Paley, a gifted early childhood teacher who has shared her classroom experiences and observations in a series of gemlike books, incorporates into the children's school experience creative drama based on their stories. In *Boys and Girls: Superheroes in the Doll Corner* (1984), she illustrates her method in a kindergarten classroom through storytelling of her own: Four boys have charged into the doll corner, "fingers shooting," disturbing the girls' domestic fantasy play:

> "You can't keep spoiling the play in the doll corner, Andrew," I say with affected calmness.
> "It's not spoiled. It's gooder this way."
> "Only if the girls agree that it's better. Tell me what you were playing and let's see if it makes a good story for me to write down." (Paley, 1984, p. 2)

Andrew tells a story of four robbers shooting people, stealing money, and then going back to their hiding places. Paley then explains the process:

> Storytelling is easy to promote when there is a tangible connection to play. Andrew's story completes the interrupted scene in the doll corner. . . . Later, with the class seated around the sixteen-foot circle we use as a stage, I read Andrew's story and ask for actors. (1984, p. 2)

Freeing children to deal with strong emotions through the safety of play and creative expression is a responsibility veteran teachers assume willingly. They realize that troubling emotions can impede the flow of children's learning as well as confound their daily lives.

Caring and Bully-Free Classrooms

To borrow from Abraham Maslow's (1968) hierarchy of needs, the climates that teachers create in their classrooms can contribute to or diminish children's sense of safety, affiliation, and actualization. The following section examines three perspectives on how best to do this, employing the insights of Catherine Lewis, Nel Noddings, and Dan Olweus.

School Bonds & Happy Memories

On the basis of her observations and teacher interviews in over 50 Japanese preschools and elementary schools over a 14-year span, Lewis (1995) proposes that "Japanese education succeeds because, early on, it meets *children's* needs—for friendship, for belonging, for opportunities to shape school life" (p. 1). Lewis contends that the efforts to make schooling an enjoyable experience early on promotes children's bonding to school for later serious study:

> What I was told, again and again, was that when schools meet the needs of the whole child—for friendship, for belonging, for contribution—children will in turn develop an emotional bond to the school. They will come to see school as a place that has their best interests at heart, and they will be motivated to do their best. (1995, p. 2)

Several elements of the school climate seemed to encourage bonding to school, contrasting markedly with practices in the United States. Most prominent of these were an absence of academic instruction and children's freedom to play. Kindergarten children, for example, spent "almost *four times* as much time in free play as their American counterparts" (Lewis, 1995, p. 1). In addition, teachers promoted bonding by emphasizing "kindness, collaboration and persistence—*not* test scores" (p. 1), frequently using small groups, and giving children authority in handling their own "disputes, lead class meetings, and shape class rules and activities" (1995, p. 1).

Implementing a school practice is relatively easy in the homogenous Japanese culture because similar values are reinforced in the home and society. Some of the classroom practices Lewis observed in Japan are transferable, however, and, indeed, are already used in part by many American teachers. For instance, the concept of cooperative learning, which calls for small group work, has gained increasing popularity over the years in the United States. Works by Aronson (1978), Slavin (1980), Johnson, Johnson, and Holubec (1994), and Kagan (1997) provide excellent guidelines. All of these researchers note that simply putting children into a group to work together is not enough. Children need to be taught how to relate to each other and what their responsibilities are, both as team members and in specific group roles (e.g., leader, recorder, peacemaker, etc.).

The key difference between the American version of small groups and those in Japan lies in their purposes. In the United States, teachers tend to use cooperative groups to promote learning. The concept is often labeled "cooperative learning," and in some models competition between teams is incorporated to increase students' motivation to learn. In the small groups that Lewis observed in Japan, on the other hand, competition was avoided and social and affective growth were promoted. The use of reflection, or *hansei*, in the Japanese small groups placed deliberate attention on the affective dimension. As Lewis (1995) observed:

> After group activities, group members often reflected on the quality of their cooperation. . . . The aim of reflection went well beyond social skills, to the very values children brought to group life and the strength of children's bonds to one another. As one teacher said, children's "whole way of looking at one another changed" as they reflected on help and kindness offered by classmates. (pp. 90-91)

The Japanese teachers' desire for children's bonding was also evident when they discussed discipline problems. They emphasized understanding over compliance and attributed the best intentions to misbehaving children. For instance, when a child was about to throw a rock at a classmate, one teacher showed the child that the rock was hard and said that surely his goal was not to hurt his classmate. When Lewis asked the teachers about misbehaving children, she reported that "they transformed my questions about discipline to discussions of the teacher-child bond and the bonds among children" (1995, p. 135). This was shown in their reactions to videos of American classrooms:

> They expressed concern about many disciplinary techniques commonly used in American classrooms: writing the names of disruptive children on the blackboard, warning children that they might lose a privilege, and publicly calling attention to an individual's misbehavior. Japanese teachers worried that these techniques might humiliate and stigmatize the children most in need of deeper bonds to the group. (1995, p. 137)

Caring Classrooms. U.S. educator and philosopher Nel Noddings works in a similar vein. She urges teachers to create caring classrooms and proposes that "we should educate all our children not only for competence but also for caring. Our aim should be to encourage the growth of competent, caring, loving, and lovable people" (1992, p. xiv).

In her book *The Challenge To Care in Schools: An Alternative Approach to Education,* Noddings outlines four components of moral education. The first is modeling: "We have to show how to care in our own relations with cared-fors" (1992, p. 22). Such modeling must be mindful and pervasive, however. In an interview with the author, Noddings offered the following advice for teachers:

> Keep reflecting on everything you do to see whether, in fact, what you do does promote the growth of loving, lovable, competent, and caring people. When you examine everything you do—how you grade, the rules you make—from this perspective, you will change the way you operate.

Teachers thus model caring in the way they structure classroom procedures and teach, as well as in the way they treat children.

The second element is dialogue, which Noddings defines as being more than talking or having a conversation. "Dialogue is open-ended . . . neither party knows at the outset what the outcome or decision will be. As parents and teachers, we cannot enter into dialogue with children when we know that our decision is already made" (1992, p. 23). Such artificial discussions can be frustrating to children and counterproductive to establishing a caring climate. In contrast, the true dialogue Nodding describes results in respect and appreciation for the other person.

The third element is practice. We need to spend time in school on teaching caring, just as we designate time for teaching other subjects. As Noddings points out, "If we decide that the capacity to care is as much a mark of personhood as reason or rationality, then we will want to find ways to increase this capacity" (1992, p. 24). Noddings applauds service learning as one means of encouraging caring through practice, with the caveat that the attitude needs to be taught along with the action.

For the fourth element, Noddings draws on Buber's (1965) concept of confirmation, describing it as "an act of affirming and encouraging the best in others. When we confirm someone, we spot a better self and encourage its development" (1992, p. 25). This is similar to the philosophy held by the Japanese teachers Lewis observed, who attributed the best intentions to misbehaving children. As Noddings observes, "Confirmation lifts us toward our vision of a better self" (1992, p. 25).

These four elements—modeling, dialogue, practice, and confirmation—can enhance the quality of communication and behavior in a classroom and create a more caring environment for children. In such classrooms, children can find refuge from the stress in their homes and other social environments.

Bully-free Classrooms. Creating a bully-free environment is another means of providing a safe and caring classroom. Bullying is a very real and frightening problem for children, but one that adults tend to overlook or minimize. Dan Olweus (1993), who conducted a series of extensive studies of bullying in Sweden and Norway, reports that about 15 percent of students in primary and junior high schools in Norway were involved in bully/victim problems—as victims, bullies, or both victims and bullies. He estimated that other countries have similar, if not higher, rates. Students in his studies reported that teachers and parents seemed unaware of bullying and did little to intervene.

Two findings from these studies are poignantly relevant to people in the United States, who have too often witnessed the horror of armed students taking the lives of schoolmates and teachers on school campuses. First, Olweus classifies one group in his studies as both victims and bullies. Many of the U.S. perpetrators of school violence were social outcasts bullied by student athletes and members of other "in groups." The perpetrators switched from victim to bully with the aid of weapons. As we seek preventive measures against the re-occurrence of such violence, we must examine bullying and the alienation, anger, and despair it causes.

The second disturbing finding in Olweus's studies is the tie between bullying in childhood and criminal activity in young adulthood. He reports that "approximately 60 percent of boys who were characterized as bullies in grades 6-9 had at least one [criminal] conviction by the age of 24" (1993, p. 36). Clearly, eliminating bullying in elementary school benefits the bullies as well as their victims.

The good news Olweus offers is that intervention programs can reduce bullying significantly. In one of his studies, in which 2,500 boys and girls in grades 4 to 7 were involved in an intervention program, bullying was reduced by at least 50 percent. The effects were lasting and even more pronounced after two years. In addition, Olweus found "a clear reduction in general antisocial behavior such as vandalism, fighting, theft, drunkenness, and truancy . . . [and] improved order and discipline, more positive social relationships, and a more positive attitude to schoolwork and the school" (p. 113).

The initial steps for an intervention program are raising awareness; defining bullying behavior clearly;

administering a questionnaire on bullying to teachers, parents, and students; and establishing clear school-wide rules against bullying. Olweus suggests posting and following these rules:

1. We shall not bully other students.
2. We shall try to help students who are bullied.
3. We shall make a point to include students who become easily left out. (1993, p. 82)

Several guiding principles support such interventions:

> [To] create a school (and ideally, also a home) environment characterized by warmth, positive interest, and involvement from adults on one hand and firm limits to unacceptable behavior on the other. . . . In cases of violations of limits and rules, nonhostile, nonphysical sanctions should be consistently applied. . . . Finally, adults are to act as authorities at least in some respects. (Olweus, 1993, p. 115)

The authoritative, rather than authoritarian (Baumrind, 1971), model of adult-child interaction is to be followed. (In the former, children's views are considered before the adult makes a final decision. In the latter, the adult's word is law and not to be questioned or discussed.) Success for these interventions, Olweus asserts, begins with awareness, commitment, and active teacher (and preferably also parent) participation.

Ways To Explore Schoolchildren's Stress

How can teachers better understand the conditions of children's lives and the degree of stress they experience? Knowing and understanding students is at the heart of all good teaching, so it is not the question that is new but rather its focus. How can classroom teachers discover children's levels and sources of stress?

Children's Home Life

Veteran teachers will attest that spending time with a child's parent can be enlightening. I recall worrying about a 6th-grade student who, I assumed, was having problems because she spoke so little in class and with her peers. I looked forward to discussing my concern with her mother during a parent conference. When we met, I almost immediately gained some valuable insight. To each question I asked, the mother would reply with only a single word or single phrase. However, through the brief replies it became clear that the woman was a fine mother, and her daughter was well-adjusted and engaged in a variety of activities that many children her age enjoy. After I pressed the mother to expand upon her answers (no doubt one time too many), she sighed and matter-of-factly said, "We don't believe in a lot of wasted talk in our family."

A colleague who has taught more than 30 years in an elementary school in a poor urban community visits each of his students at home before the school year begins. While seated at the kitchen table, he expresses appreciation for having the child in his class and discusses with the parent(s) the child's personal and academic goals for the coming year. Sometimes, older siblings are engaged in drug- or gang-related activities in the next room, but my colleague remains focused on the child who will be in his class. The purpose of his visit, he explains, is not to investigate the family but rather to welcome the child, learn about him or her, and begin a relationship with the parent(s).

Teachers also find a variety of ways to form partnerships with parents. Some have a parent group assist in the classroom or prepare materials; others invite parents and grandparents to share a favorite children's literature book with the class. Some elicit parents' help with field trips, class projects, and celebrations; others invite families to award, drama, or musical programs. Teachers can partner regularly with parents through newsletters, interactive homework assignments, and positive phone calls about their child's good behavior or accomplishments. Arranging for, and teaching, special classes for adults—on parenting, grandparenting, family math, and English or other language classes—are other ways teachers can connect with their students' families. Teachers who see students in the context of their family lives gain insights on their strengths, concerns, and sources of stress.

Children's School Lives

Teachers can learn about children's stress by reading their creative writing and journal assignments. Dialogue journals, in which teachers reply to children's entries with entries of their own, offer information about how children view their lives, learning, and stress. Although time-consuming, this type of journal can be particularly helpful when teachers are puzzled by students' behaviors and attitudes.

Researching children's school experiences though teacher-developed questionnaires and sociograms also can be instructive. For young students, teachers can read the questions orally and direct children to respond by marking smiling, neutral, or frowning faces on their questionnaires. Older children can reply by writing short responses to a few key questions, such as what are they looking forward to doing, what ways they prefer to study, what problems they wish the teacher would solve, etc. Teachers may use or adapt Olweus's Bully/Victim Questionnaire (see this chapter's list of "Suggested Readings").

Sociograms help teachers examine social networks, relationships, and students' sphere of influence in the classroom. Either in brief individual interviews or through a questionnaire, teachers create sociograms by asking children to give their first, second, and third choices of classmates in responses to several questions, such as "Whom would you choose to sit by on the bus on the fieldtrip?" "Whom would you choose to work with on our science project?" Teachers tally the children's choices on a grid that lists the names of all children in the class on both the vertical and the horizontal axes. Weighting the first, second, and third choices, they total the points each child received. Teachers then create, for themselves, classroom social maps or diagrams, using circles with children's names and arrows and lines to other circles with children's names to indicate their choices. In the process, teachers discover the isolated, the social stars, and the friendship networks in the class. After uncovering stress-producing social interaction patterns, the teacher can make adjustments to alleviate any problems. Hubbard and Power offer specific directions for conducting sociograms and provide helpful illustrations in their book *The Art of Classroom Inquiry: A Handbook for Teacher-Researchers* (1993).

Tending to Their Own Stress

As a university teacher who works with a number of graduate students in their first years of teaching in Southern California, I know they encounter multiple layers of stress. First are the graduate students' personal stresses—juggling their activities and time according to their roles as teachers, spouses, parents, and graduate students. Second are the stresses they encounter in their classrooms—curricular mandates, state testing pressures, and the presence of students with a more extensive range of native languages, cultural diversity, academic experience, and ability levels than ever before. Third are the stresses they encounter through their troubled students and parents, as described in Part I of this book. Fourth are the stresses many encounter because of the contrast between their own school and life experiences and those of their students.

The experience of a student in my "Research for Educators" class provides a good example of the fourth type of stress. She was dangerously close to burnout in her second year of teaching. A white middle class student, she grew up in a two-parent family that valued education, working hard, and love for one another. She worked conscientiously in school, achieved good grades, and attended college on a swimming scholarship. In her research report, she described the school where she taught, which contrasted dramatically with her own:

> The school was 90 percent Hispanic, 5 percent African American, 3 percent Asian, 2 percent white. Most students came from single-parent families headed by women whose annual incomes were less than $10,000. In my 1st-grade classroom I had 20 students, three of whom had a two-parent family. Many of my students lived in motels with three to four siblings and [they] did not have food available to them. The students came from homes where emotional and physical abuse was prevalent. Several times I had to call child services to check out child endangerment situations. I had 17 students below grade level [who] were low functioning. Four of my students received speech therapy two days a week and seven were on modified reading programs. All the students I worked with struggled with neglect, poverty, and abuse. Unfortunately these children had to bear the burden of adult issues at such an early age [at a point] where they had no control over changing their situations.

Such discrepancies in life experiences can baffle, anger, and stress teachers as they attempt to understand needs and values so different from their own.

Individually or in combination, these four types of stressors can drive novice teachers away from our profession before they have truly begun. It is not surprising that Linda Darling Hammond (1998) found attrition rates for beginning teachers to be about 30 percent during the first three to five years of teaching (p. 8). In urban schools where stress is aggravated by poverty, the pace of beginning teacher attrition is faster.

Advice From Teachers in Stressed Environments

In two related studies that explored the perspectives of positive, persevering veteran teachers who worked in some of the most distressed urban environments in the U.S., I sought explanations for their resiliency and advice to help novice teachers persevere (Stanford, 2000, 2001). The participants in both studies attributed their resiliency to their commitment to making a difference in children's lives; the support of family, friends, and colleagues; and personal or spiritual reservoirs of strength. Many had persevered through other stressful life experiences, including racial prejudice and violent deaths of family members; as a consequence, they knew that they could handle stress. Some persisted in their work because they enjoyed it and felt they did it well.

Their advice for novice teachers entering similarly stressed environments fell into four broad areas: 1) teach in that environment for the right reasons, 2) have realistic expectations, 3) be educationally prepared, and 4) focus on the children. Being prepared for stress buffers its impact. One teacher warned, "Realize that some of the parents may not have the educational background, the social graces that maybe you're accustomed to . . . [and they will be] in your face for whatever reason." She handled such situations by recognizing that parents, like their children, needed attention. She continued, "So you give the parents that attention . . . find out what it is that they really want," and then "they become your biggest ally" (Stanford, 1999).

In addition, the teachers mentioned the familiar modes of avoiding burnout. Some recommended escaping: broadening their lives, taking classes, getting away, going on quick vacations, reading, tapping their sense of humor, doing aerobics, enjoying hobbies, sleeping, listening to music, taking a year off, and "pulling back and getting a life." Some fought stress by making changes: changing the way they did things, changing grade levels, and attending "good inservices" and workshops to learn new strategies. And some avoided burnout by looking inward: slowing down, evaluating what matters, "understanding why you're there," and "finding a way to make it worthwhile."

Control, Commitment, and Challenge

Kobasa (1979) proposed that people's hardiness—their ability to resist stress—is strengthened by their sense of control in life circumstances, their perception of stressful events as being challenges rather than threats, and their personal sense of commitment. When they feel overwhelmed, teachers can benefit by stepping back and deliberately regaining a sense of control. Three ways to do this are by evaluating and categorizing their stress, eliminating unnecessary demands, and prioritizing the remaining ones. They also gain control by working directly on some of the problems stressing them. The student in the research class chose to do case studies on three of her most needy (and stressful to her) students. In the process, her frustration with them gradually transformed to compassion, and her distress lessened.

Another means of becoming a hardy teacher is by regarding the stress involved in teaching as a challenge rather than a threat. The career-persevering urban teachers were positive because they believed that they were good teachers. None expressed concerns about not doing their jobs well. For novice teachers who feel overwhelmed and wonder how they will manage, the veterans suggested that they find a soul mate or mentor to help them. "Remember the word 'help' . . . just remember that we all were beginning teachers and there were things we didn't know," one advised. Recalling the first days of her teaching career, which began with a class that was out of control after being taught by a series of substitute teachers, one of the career-persevering teachers illustrated such advice well: "After three days I was walking down the hall crying, and somebody pulled me in and said, 'Have you called their parents?' I said, 'No.' And that took care of it." Transforming the threat into a challenge is sometimes simply a matter of seeking help from an effective, experienced teacher.

Being committed to making a difference in the lives of children is what spurred on the veteran urban teachers. They believed that their students could learn in spite of the barriers erected by their life circumstances, and that they could help them do so. Some persevered in teaching solely because they saw themselves as the last hope for many of their students.

Being committed to themselves, taking care of themselves, is also important for teachers. As Sylvia Marshall (1963) observed:

> To control a class in freedom, to learn with each child instead of instructing a passive class, to be a well of clear water into which the children can dip all the time, instead of a hosepipe dousing them with facts, is the most exhausting way of doing a teacher's job. (p. 41)

Good teaching is exhausting. Yet if teachers are drained by the endeavor, they will have little to offer. Taking time to replenish their spirits is essential. The Ginos, Pams, and others like them, who are stressed by life and developmental factors beyond their control, count on them and seek the haven of their classrooms.

"Mrs. Barth Used To Tell Us . . ."

The novelist John Barth once compared the influence of an author to that of a teacher (favorably comparing the latter to the former). In a tribute to teachers, and in particular to his wife, an English teacher, Barth explained that long after what he had written had gone out of print, his wife's students would still remember her: "A first-rate teacher's immortality is neither more nor less than the words (spoken even decades later by her former students to their own students, spouses, children, friends): "Mrs. Barth used to tell us . . ." (1987, p. 181).

Teachers, student teachers, therapists, and all adults who work with children have opportunities to assist students when they encounter stress in their personal development, school situations, or life circumstances. At such times, the adults' influence can be particularly valuable and enduring. The life lessons they teach, the reassurance they give, and the belief in children they show can be timeless gifts. To work in a field where such gift giving is possible is a high calling and the reason so many of us persevere in our challenging profession.

References

Aronson, Elliot. (1978). *The jigsaw classroom.* Beverly Hills, CA: Sage.

Ashton-Warner, Sylvia. (1963). *Teacher.* New York: Bantam Books.

Barth, John. (1987). Teacher. In L. D. Rubin, Jr. (Ed.), *An apple for my teacher* (pp. 161-181). Chapel Hill, NC: Algonquin Books of Chapel Hill.

Baumrind, Diana. (1971). Current patterns of parental authority. *Developmental Psychology Monographs, 4* (1, Pt. 2).

Brim, Gilbert. (1992). *Ambition.* New York: Basic Books.

Buber, Martin. (1965). Education. In Martin Buber (Ed.), *Between man and man* (pp. 83-103). New York: Macmillan.

Darling-Hammond, Linda. (1998). Teachers and teaching: Testing policy hypotheses from a national commission report. *Educational Researcher, 27*(1), 5-15.

Elkind, David. (1998). *All grown up and no place to go: Teenagers in crisis* (Rev. ed.). Reading, MA: Addison-Wesley.

Hubbard, Ruth Shagoury, & Power, Brenda Miller. (1993). *The art of classroom inquiry: A handbook for teacher-researchers.* Portsmouth, NH: Heinemann.

Jackson, Philip W. (1968). *Life in classrooms.* New York: Holt.

Johnson, David W., Johnson, Roger T., & Holubec, Edythe J. (1994). *Cooperative learning in the classroom.* Alexandria, VA: Association for Supervision and Curriculum Development.

Kagan, Spencer. (1997). *Cooperative learning.* Riverside, CA: Kagan Cooperative Learning.

Kobasa, Susan. (1979). Stressful life events, personality, and health: An inquiry into hardiness. *Journal of Personality and Social Psychology, 37*(1), 1-11.

Kounin, Jacob Sebastian. (1970). *Discipline and group management in classrooms.* New York: Holt.

Lewis, Catherine C. (1995). *Educating hearts and minds: Reflections on Japanese preschool and elementary education.* New York: Cambridge University Press.

Marshall, Sybil. (1963). *An experiment in education.* London: Cambridge University Press.

Maslow, Abraham H. (1968). *Toward a psychology of being* (2nd ed.). New York: Van Nostrand Reinhold.

Noddings, Nel. (1992). *The challenge to care in schools: An alternative approach to education.* New York: Teachers College Press.

Olweus, Dan. (1993). *Bullying at school: What we know and what we can do.* Cambridge, MA: Blackwell.

Paley, Vivian Gussin. (1984). *Boys and girls: Superheroes in the doll corner.* Chicago: University of Chicago Press.

Slavin, Robert E. (1980). Cooperative learning. *Review of Educational Research, 50*(2), 315-345.

Stanford, Beverly Hardcastle. (1999, April). *Tapping the wisdom of positive, persevering teachers: The South Central L.A. study.* Paper presented at the annual meeting of the American Educational Research Association, Montreal, Canada.

Stanford, Beverly Hardcastle. (2000, May). *Advice from the trenches: Insights from urban teachers with high morale and career perseverance.* Paper presented at the Coventry University Qualitative Evidence-based Practice Conference, Coventry, England.

Stanford, Beverly Hardcastle. (2001). Reflections of resilient, persevering urban teachers. *Teacher Education Quarterly, 28*(3), 75-87.

Wassermann, Selma. (1992). Professional teachers deal with children "in trouble." *Childhood Education, 68,* 232-233.

Wood, David. (1988, 1998). *How children think and learn: The social contexts of cognitive development* (2nd ed.). Malden, MA: Blackwell Publishers.

Suggested Readings and Resources for Teachers

Responses to Children's Stress

Carmichael, Lucianne Bond. (1981). *McDonogh 15: Becoming a school.* New York: Avon Books.

Dreikurs, Rudolf. (1972). *Discipline without tears.* New York: Hawthorne Books.

Elkind, David. (1994). *Ties that stress: The new family imbalance.* Cambridge, MA: Harvard University Press.

Garbarino, James. (1995). *Raising children in a socially toxic environment.* San Francisco: Jossey-Bass.

Marshall, Sybil. (1966). *An experiment in education.* New York: Cambridge University Press.

Nelsen, Jane. (1981, 1987). *Positive discipline.* New York: Ballantine.
Paley, Vivian. (1995). *Kwanzaa and me: A teacher's story.* Cambridge, MA: Harvard University Press.
Paley, Vivian. (2000). *The kindness of children.* Cambridge, MA: Harvard University Press.
Payne, Ruby K. (1998). *A framework for understanding poverty.* Highlands, TX: Aha! Process, Inc. (www.rftpub.com)
Stailey, Jay C., & Payne, Ruby K. (1998). *Think rather of zebras: Dealing with aspects of poverty through story.* Highlands, TX: Aha! Process, Inc. (www.rftpub.com)
Yamamoto, Kaoru. (1993). *Their world, our world: Reflections on childhood.* Westport, CT: Praeger.

Caring and Bully-free Classrooms

Beane, Allan L. (1999). *The bully free classroom: Over 100 tips and strategies for teachers K-8.* Minneapolis, MI: Free Spirit Publishing Inc. (www.freespirit.com)
Developmental Studies Center. (1995). *Homeside activities: Conversations and activities that bring parents into children's schoolside learning.* Oakland, CA: Developmental Studies Center. 800-666-7270. (Take-home activities in English and Spanish.)
Lewis, Catherine C. (1995). *Educating hearts and minds: Reflections on Japanese preschool and elementary education.* New York: Cambridge University Press.
Noddings, Nel. (1992). *The challenge to care in schools: An alternative approach to education.* New York: Teachers College Press.
Olweus, Dan. (1993). *Bullying at school: What we know and what we can do.* Cambridge, MA: Blackwell.
Paley, Vivian. (1992). *You can't say you can't play.* Cambridge, MA: Harvard University Press.
Wagner, Betty Jane. (Ed.). (1999). *Building moral communities through educational drama.* Stamford, CT: Ablex.

For Children

Allard, Harry. (1977). *Miss Nelson is missing.* Boston: Houghton Mifflin. Upper Elementary. Children's misbehavior in class drives their teacher away and brings in a tough substitute, Miss Nelson in disguise.
Bishop, Clarie Huchet. (1978). *Twenty and ten.* New York: Puffin. Upper Elementary. A group of 20 children hide and protect 10 Jewish children from Nazi soldiers.
Blume, Judy. (1986). *It's not the end of the world.* New York: Yearling. Upper Elementary. A girl struggles with her parents' fighting and likely divorce.
Bunting, Eva. (1993). *Fly away home.* New York: Clarion. Upper Elementary. The homeless experiences of a boy and his father.
Bradley, Kimberly Brubaker. (1999). *Ruthie's gift.* New York: Delacorte Press. Upper Elementary. The family and school trials of an 8-year old girl.
Cleary, Beverly. (1984). *Dear Mr. Henshaw.* New York: Dell. Upper Elementary. A boy finds help through writing about his troubles.
de Paola, Tomie. (1997). *Nana Upstairs and Nana Downstairs.* New York: Putnam. For ages 4-8. A child grieves over the death of a great grandmother.
Kraus, Joseph. (1971). *Leo, the late bloomer.* New York: Windmill. Primary Grades. Leo grows at his own pace.
Patterson, Katherine. (1977). *Bridge to Terabithia.* New York: Crowell. Upper Elementary. A book about children's gender stereotypes, special friendships, and a child's death.
Rylant, Cynthia. (1992). *Missing May.* New York: Orchard. Young adult. A child finds a loving family, loses a dear aunt, and learns to heal.
Wells, Rosemary. (2000). *Timothy goes to school.* New York: Viking. Primary Grades. Timothy encounters the ups and downs of going to school.

Author's Note

The author expresses appreciation to Monica DeMott and Lori Anderson Klassen, two young urban teachers—one in Norfolk, Virginia, and the other in Monta Vista, California—who kindly read and responded to an earlier version of this chapter.

Chapter 8
From the Therapy Room

Sherry Lawry Young

A young mother, her tension apparent, was explaining her reason for calling the office. Despite her quick, choppy speech, she did her best to outline the problem. "My son's teacher has been suggesting that I get him 'professional help.' "

Natalie (all case studies are composites and all names have been changed) explained that her 7-year-old son Mac never wanted to go to school, instead always asking his mother if he could stay home with her. Mac was having a hard time concentrating in class and keeping his hands to himself. He was disruptive and often mean. Although his teacher knew Mac was bright, the work he handed in was often incomplete and sloppy. This morning, Natalie had received a call from the school. Mac had used a pen to rip his pants, cutting through to the skin. His insistence that it was an accident notwithstanding, Mac's mother and teacher were concerned. "Could someone see my boy today?" Natalie pleaded.

Thus began my relationship with Mac and his family. An attentive teacher detected the signs of distress in a youngster's unwillingness to settle down. Because of that teacher's suggestion, her student and his family would receive help. As the counseling relationship developed, Mac's story began to unfold. Natalie had been in one abusive relationship after another. Mac not only had seen his mother pushed and hit by various men, but also once acted to rescue her. During a party, as Natalie's partner attempted to stuff her into a car trunk, Mac picked up a heavy shovel and stopped the assault on his mother with one swing to the back of the man's heel. After that night, this 7-year-old had taken on the role of defender and protector of his family. He could not bear to be separated from his mother for long. He had to keep watch.

As he revealed later, his last encounter with his biological father had been a painful one. Months earlier, the visit had ended with Mac's father saying, "Get him out of here. He's not even mine." Mac was never allowed to sort out that confusing confrontation; he simply never saw his father again. The play therapy room gave Mac his first opportunity to explore all that had happened and what he was feeling. He worked on his confusion and anger by playing out metaphorical scenes in a nonjudgmental atmosphere, exploring all that terrorized him. I was not there to correct or teach; instead, I walked beside him as he uncovered each fear, threat, and disappointment. I would be his witness.

Inside of Mac was a frightened boy, the family protector, and a youngster who felt disdain for all adults. All these roles were juggling for position as he spent his days in a classroom, expected to conform and learn. Because Mac did not have the words, he demonstrated the pain he was experiencing by injuring himself. This time it worked. He got noticed and received the help he needed. Many children do not.

Mac's story is one example of the stressors that children face and bring with them into the classroom every day. Although often invisible, these burdens are carried in on shoulders too narrow to withstand the weight. The stressors often manifest themselves in undesirable behaviors and attitudes that disguise the underlying pain the child feels. Fortunately, Mac's teacher understood what a counselor could offer a family in need, as in this case. Families referred to counseling have much work ahead of them, but they can be successful.

My Pilgrimage

As a counselor and program director of a small nonprofit agency called Bridge Builders Counseling, Inc., I work exclusively with poor, one-parent families. The majority of my clients are children under age 16, most of whom are abused, neglected, abandoned, and impoverished. I earned a master's degree in counseling with the intent of working in the area of adult grief therapy. It was during my internship at Oakland University, in Rochester, Michigan, that an encounter with a small child from a chaotic home convinced me that working with children through non-directive play therapy was where my heart and talent lay. My job description and clientele are different than I envisioned when I began work on my degree, but I find that I am indeed working with grief and loss issues as I listen to these children tell their painful stories.

What I find most rewarding about working at Bridge Builders is that we offer a professional service that might otherwise be inaccessible to this special population. Incorporated in 1994, this small agency provides individual and family counseling, networking within the community, and mentoring relationships for boys being raised without fathers. We counsel approximately 80 families per year, and we teach prevention education courses in the community.

My admiration for the children I work with grows with each session. Given the opportunity, youngsters learn how to communicate their unnamed feelings and rediscover the self-esteem that years of abuse have eroded. I see a resiliency in these youngsters that will help them recover from their losses. But resiliency does not mean that these children or their parents are indestructible. In many cases, the damage that has been done will not be erased with mere attention or education. These families carry heavy baggage created by years of abuse, and they are extremely vulnerable to falling back on unhealthful coping skills and returning to the all-too-familiar abusive patterns. The hardships of poverty, conflict, violence, and uncertainty all take their toll.

While working with children every day, continually learning about and practicing the techniques of play therapy, I am aware that the process of counseling children is often unclear to those outside my office. This fact becomes obvious when a troubled child is sent to me with the request to have his or her problem behavior "fixed," or when I am asked to "get the truth out of him." What typically happens when children and their families enter therapy (often because a teacher has suggested that a child needs the additional help) is very different from a "fix." In its purest form, play therapy provides the child with a safe place for him or her to examine and work on issues, and a witness to their story. The witness offers understanding and a willingness to enter into the pain, and provides guidance as the relationship develops.

The story of Mac and his mother is not unlike other cases seen by our agency. These families come from a world of poverty, abuse, abandonment, and neglect that often reaches back generations. Emery (1999) lists the four most pronounced stressors for children in one-parent families. The first, and most intrusive, is poverty; according to Emery, 52 percent of families living at or below the poverty level are headed by females. The other stressors are lack of contact with the absent parent, the poor quality of the parent/child relationship, and conflict between the child's biological parents. Poverty not only causes the most stress for children being raised by a single parent, it also frequently means the family does not take advantage of mental health services. Mac was a rare exception. For him, the play therapy allowed him to gradually come to terms with his experiences. In the months that followed, he would sort out his life. Once they know they have permission to explore their feelings, some children find the strength to regain self-esteem and learn how to make healthful choices.

Each of us is born with a natural ability to adapt to life's stress and strain. Children tap into this ability in order to sit in their classroom and learn their lessons after experiencing a night of neglect or abuse. As Elkind (1981) points out, however, their ability to adapt is diminished when they are continuously bombarded with acute distress and do not have the opportunity to recover. Signs of overload come in many forms; frantic overachievement and a reversion to infantile behavior are just two signs of distress in a child who lacks the words to express his or her feelings.

Karr-Morse and Wiley (1997) examined the impact of continuous stress on the development of the child's brain. "Under conditions of extreme threat or rage, when the brain is flooded with stress hormones, the 'fight or flight' human is not under the governance of the analytical cortex, the seat of rationality and wisdom. Under those extreme conditions, it is the limbic brain and midbrain which are quickest to respond to mobilize the individual" (p. 33). Using the metaphor of a soldier being trained for battle, the authors explain that the emphasis on learning to instantly react to any emergency does not leave the child an opportunity to enhance analytical thinking. Instead, the child's brain develops basic survival instincts, while the higher functions are left understimulated and less accessible.

The children I see in the play therapy room can neither mask painful feelings nor be confident that they can handle their circumstances. When these feelings are left unaddressed, irreparable damage can take place, both to the children and the adults caring for them (Miller, 1981).

The type of caring we offer to the children we meet in the therapy room is not sentimental. Axline (1964), a pioneer in the field of child therapy, reminds us that caring is not consolation and affection. Rather, caring means helping a child to live in the world he knows, and helping him find the resources, within himself and around him, that will help him cope with his problems.

We can look to Moustakas as an excellent source for educators seeking to connect with stressed children. Although speaking specifically to counselors, Moustakas (1975) inspires a broader audience with his metaphorical language of connecting:

> It is essential to be open to the unique features of each relationship, to be free to follow what actually exists, however different, strange, or unlike other moments . . . to be responsive to one's own self and the specific person who has come to seek help. . . . The essential thing in therapy is just this response to the unknown, this freedom to enter in and begin a real life with other persons not determined or limited by any preconceived notions, the freedom to let a specific relationship be its own thing and to go with it. What emerges is an attitude like that of a child standing at the seashore with open arms stretching forward, ready to receive the crash of waves or the gentle lapping of the water. What also emerges is a process of affecting and being affected by others. (pp. 133-134)

Counseling As a Caring Community

We are all meant to be in a community. An encouraging, celebrating community reflects back to children a vision of what they can be, and stands with them as they explore the shame, loneliness, and fear that sometimes get in the way of that vision. A true community offers patience as each child decides what to keep and what to discard, as they work to transform anger and self-pity into hope and self-worth.

The counseling session is a miniature rendition of a caring community; it is a safe haven during the process of healing, and play therapy is a specific technique through which a child can effectively communicate. Play therapy was introduced by Hug-Hellmuth in 1919 and soon recognized as a valid psychoanalytic technique, distinct from child therapy (Gil, 1991). Based on Roger's client-centered therapy, Axline (1964) developed non-directive play therapy in the 1940s as a specific approach to therapy with children, leaving "the responsibility and direction to the child" (p. 9).

Sweeney (1997) explains that children thrive in an atmosphere that offers safety and security, and in which the child's language is spoken. The language children speak most fluently is play, through which children show that imagination is not only a natural coping skill, but also a healing agent. If distressed children did not play, they might not survive.

Entering a young child's world conveys respect and honor. It sends a message that the counselor cares about what the child has to say and is willing to take the time to understand. Our willingness to get involved in play will not be wasted on the child. Giving control of the relationship to the child will provide a rare confidence-building experience. This concept of entering into a child's world of play, rather than expecting that the child will seek ways to relate to us, is a basic tenet of community.

Consistency is another valuable element of play therapy. The predictable amount of time spent together each week, the attention of the counselor, the reliability of the relationship, and even the room itself provide an environment the child can learn to trust. A troubled child may tentatively explore the room during the first months of therapy; he might, for example, at first play with only one ball from a room full of toys, tossing it back and forth with his counselor. This is the child's first step toward a trusting relationship with the counselor.

It is helpful for the child to know that the special relationship he develops with his counselor will not change no matter what he reveals. He can regard his counselor as a special helping friend. In this relationship, unlike most others the young child has had with an adult, questions will not be raised, problem behaviors will not be presented and solved, and discipline will not be delivered. Instead, the child learns that change will be in his or her hands. While it is tempting for the counselor to analyze and interpret what the sessions reveal, the counselor's job is simply to witness the process for the child (Sweeney, 1997).

Play therapy, by its very nature, is sometimes viewed as slow, unstructured, and of little value to those parents and teachers who believe that counseling should "fix the behavior" of a distressed child. Nevertheless, play has long been recognized as the means by which children master problem-solving, social, and competency skills. Given the opportunity to "play it out," children are more likely to gain control of fears and anxieties, both real and imagined. When we remember that their behavior is only a symptom of the underlying problem, and that they have the ability to heal themselves when given a safe place, we can allow play to be a child's expression of feelings (Gil, 1991).

A case in point was illustrated in *Dibs: In Search of Self* by Axline (1964). Dibs, a 5-year-old client, tentatively entered into play therapy. After two years, Dibs emerges with a strong sense of self that might not have been possible without the warm safety of play therapy. Although the child in this case was from a wealthy family, the story is one we also can apply to a child in poverty. The isolation of the child, the inability of the parents to cope with his special needs, and the frustration of teachers who could not offer special attention to one troubled student are the same, no matter what the economic background. As Dibs's story unfolds, we witness an amazing journey to self-discovery. Each week, young Dibs explores his fear and hurt through play. His companion on the journey does not guide or teach, but rather reflects. Entering into his world only as Dibs permits, she provides the space and security for him to discover his own strength.

This is not to say that there is no structure or theoretical principles involved in play therapy. According to Norton and Norton (1997), counselors will observe a general progression of 1) exploration; 2) testing, as trust develops; 3) expression of the challenges facing the child, as the counselor witnesses and perhaps is invited to enter into the struggle; 4) growth, as the child finds mastery over the problem; and 5) separation, as the counselor witnesses the child releasing his or her intense feelings concerning the issue. At this point, children may move on to another issue or indicate they are ready to terminate therapy. Children learn that when they express their feelings, the counselor will merely reflect those feelings back and convey to the children that they have the power to overcome the challenges they face. The counselor is careful not to label or direct anything that happens in a session; he or she conveys patience and attention to any activity or conversation.

A Case Study of Finding Strength From Tragedy

One fall evening a young mother, Rhonda, brought in her 6-year-old son for an initial therapy session. Thomas had just started 1st grade. According to his teacher, Thomas was having a tough time adjusting to his new surroundings. Because of his increasingly violent outbursts, the teacher suggested that Rhonda seek a professional counselor.

Rhonda worked part-time as a hairdresser; to help make ends meet, she and her son were living with her mother in a small apartment. They were not the only ones living there; Thomas's aunt, two cousins, and his step-grandfather also lived in the apartment. Thomas and the two other boys all slept together in one bed. According to her report, Rhonda would spend most nights at her boyfriend's house, where there was more room, and return each morning in time to get her son off to school.

Although it wasn't really "quality time," Thomas's father had seen his son every weekend since the divorce. Rhonda appreciated any help she could get from the father in handling their active child; the stress was often unbearable. Rhonda was enraged, however, by her ex-husband's most recent action. Six weeks earlier, he abruptly moved to Kentucky to start a new business. Not only was he suddenly out of Thomas' life, he didn't say good-bye before he left and hadn't made contact since. Thomas had become increasingly aggressive each day. Rhonda reported that Thomas was throwing things and hitting and biting anything that got in his way. When his teacher became aware of the father's absence, he suggested getting additional help for Thomas.

Tragedy followed tragedy. Two days after that initial session, Rhonda's mother called our office to tell us that her daughter had died of a gunshot wound. She wanted to let us know she would keep the appointment her daughter had made, but thought we should know what had happened before they came in.

In the year that followed, through nondirective play therapy, Thomas was able to find a safe place to explore the losses in his life. Because he could not articulate his pain and confusion, Thomas used "play [as his] language . . . and toys [for his] words" (Sweeney, 1997, p. 71). Never fully able to grasp the complexity of the tragedy in his life, this young boy expressed some of his fear and deep sadness by using angry story lines and intense role-playing.

One day, as Thomas led us again into our usual unique story line of a caregiver/son who beats up all the other characters in the story, he suddenly grew very quiet. As he lay across a chair with his head under my desk, he broke the silence with a small voice I could barely hear: "Now the boy came home from school and he's all alone in the house. No one lives there anymore. And no one knows the boy is alone."

Given the opportunity, Thomas told me of his biggest fear. This child had experienced tragic losses and poverty in his six short years. At this young age, he was forced to accept what few of us face—he could lose even more, and he feared there would be no one to acknowledge that fact, or even care.

Now, Thomas is 8 and his grandmother still makes periodic appointments for him here at the Bridge Builders office. Together, they have learned to live together and support each other in their loss. During a recent session, Thomas wanted to revisit the newspaper article that told the story of his mother's death. He studied the old, worn clipping with his back to me. He was now able to understand the words that he couldn't read two years ago. We talked about what might have happened that day. Then Thomas calmly informed me that he was taking the clipping, and that if I wanted a copy, I should make one now. With the help of his grandmother we placed the newspaper clipping in an envelope and decided where to store it for safekeeping at home. While this was a rather gruesome possession for so small a boy, it gave him a tool with which to mark his mother's death, take control of the traumatic memory, and move forward. Nothing I could say to Thomas would compare to the healing that took place because he was given permission to explore the pain of his loss.

Resources for Teachers and Parents

Although I am highlighting nondirective play therapy for stressed children, there are, conservatively speaking, more than 200 documented methods of therapy with children (Straus, 1999). Therapy that focuses on creativity and movement can help the child explore and communicate feelings at a nonverbal level, as well as provide a physical outlet. Storytelling—through drama, reading, music, and art—is natural in the classroom setting, as well as in the home. The teacher will need to watch for and respond to a child communicating trauma. (This can be challenging in the midst of a busy classroom with a demanding curriculum.) Teachers can use the above-mentioned techniques as assessment tools to reinforce their recommendation that a child needs help from a counselor.

Nondirective play therapy is most effective from the time that children are able to verbally communicate until the age of 7 to 10, depending on their developmental stage. Boys and girls appear to be on equal footing in their ability to benefit from play therapy. Directed-play or talk therapy is frequently more effective once a child has reached an age of self-consciousness. Communication with an older child often comes in the form of games or activities that allow for expression and learning. The older child learns problem-solving strategies, improves communication skills, and learns ways to form healthy relationships. This work not only addresses past issues, but also helps prevent the child from repeating unhealthy responses to stress. The child is given the opportunity to learn new skills, try them out, and process the outcomes with a trusted counselor who does not judge or rate his or her efforts.

Therapy often allows a child to safely tell his or her story—the use of animal puppets, for example. Allowing the child to tell a painful story, masked in fantasy, offers a safe distance from reality. Through puppets or other storytelling tools, the child knows he or she is free to explore feelings, or back away any time it begins to feel uncomfortable. The child gains control by telling the story, and often will repeat the story for weeks, using different themes, toys, and metaphors.

Although parents are generally not invited into the play therapy room with the counselor and child, sometimes a method known as filial therapy is used. Filial therapy teaches parents to help their children express thoughts and feelings. This is not an easy process and must be monitored frequently to maintain the integrity of its purpose. It begins with the parent observing and later participating in nondirective play sessions with the child and counselor. Many children respond well to the parent's attention and may explore issues that they would not otherwise tackle (Van Fleet, 1994).

Five-year-old Rachel is a wonderful example of a child who was more than ready to tell her father about her fear of abandonment. During the very first session, Rachel's father and I witnessed her exploration of fear through play. It is unusual for a child to use meaningful metaphor without first building rapport with the counselor. Apparently, Rachel had been looking for just such an opportunity to express herself.

Her mother had left the family when Rachel was 6 weeks old; by the time Rachel was 3, her father's drug addiction had worsened to the point where he needed to stay at a treatment facility. The father did not see Rachel for over 18 months. During that time, Rachel lived in foster care; she learned to guard herself from further loss and attachment. Consequently, she remained emotionally distant upon seeing her father again. Rachel and her father began counseling in order to begin building a new relationship.

Rachel talked to us through the character of the sad, worn-out frog puppet she had selected from the shelf. Rachel told a story of the frog's mom and dad who went into the woods for a walk and never came out. The bears were now caring for the lost parents and the little frog lived alone in the yard, under some leaves, awaiting their return.

Throughout her father's absence, Rachel had been seeking an answer to her question about why her parents did not love her enough to stay. She found comfort in believing that they were lost and on their way back to her. In her early developmental stage, Rachel could find no other explanation for her parents' seemingly thoughtless abandonment.

Play therapy allowed Rachel to express her feelings and acknowledge her past, making it safe for her to explore the present. No amount of problem-solving exercises, directives, or questioning could meet her needs. Rachel most needed an opportunity to express herself and have her feelings affirmed; only then would she begin the healing process with her father. Rachel communicated the depth of her fears and longing in a way that was only possible through play.

Unfortunately, Rachel's father discontinued counseling after only a few sessions and I never heard from them again. Many parents disengage from a therapeutic relationship too soon, possibly because of any number of distractions and stressors. Many end counseling relationships at the first sign that the child's troublesome behaviors have ceased. Unfortunately, the child usually has not fully processed his or her feelings. Parents will sometimes, after only a few weeks, report to the counselor that their child is doing better in school and the teacher no longer has to give warnings. Because the child looks better and acts better, the parents want to believe that the child *is* better. The truth is, the child needs more time to explore his feelings before he is ready to end therapy. Teachers can encourage these stressed families to continue therapy even after the child's symptoms are less obvious.

Frequently, a child or parent will sabotage the healing process and abruptly change course because the family dynamics, although unhealthy, are all they know. Therapy, which strips away defenses and threatens boundaries, can be a scary process. Even the smallest child might attempt to thwart the process of healing. The counselor can respond by acknowledging the positive signs of change as well as the client's or family's desire for a return to safe territory (Tyndall-Lind, 1999).

Although the counselor may hope that helping the family gain new insights would help the healing process continue, the reality is that the family frequently ends therapy for the time being. They may begin again when they are ready. I can only hope that is what happened with Rachel and her father.

Because of family loyalty, children often are reluctant to examine abuse or neglect they may have received from those who are supposed to be nurturing them. Their resistance also could stem from self-blame; they may believe they are somehow the cause for the family's poverty and violence. Their loyalty and shame could prevent them from continuing to examine painful events (Baldwin, 1997). By collaborating with the child's counselor periodically, with the knowledge and consent of the custodial parent, the classroom teacher can offer unique insights and observations about the child, and thus be a valuable link between the child and the therapist.

Conclusion

Similar to the hard-working classroom teacher surrounded by a roomful of toys, the counselor of young children is not playing, even if that is what it looks like! The counselor has the challenge of being neither playmate nor casual observer. The effectiveness of the interaction depends on the counselor remembering his or her role at all times. The experienced counselor, like the classroom teacher, is ready to think on his or her feet and respond to whatever the child throws into the mix at any given moment, and yet not get lost in the activity or push the child too far. For both teachers and counselors, Moustakas (1966) said it best:

> Personal interaction between teacher and child means that differences in children are recognized and valued. Expression and exploration of the child's uniqueness and distinctiveness are encouraged. Only what is true and therefore of value to society can emerge from individual interests which are expressions of one's true nature. Adults may offer resources, make available opportunities and give information and help when it is meaningful to the child; but, in a personal relationship, to force standards, social values, and concepts on the child is to stifle his potential creativity and difference. (p. 33)

Despite our best efforts, the children in our care may end up in jail, get pregnant too young, or decide that rage is the only answer to their problems. Being available does not guarantee that the children will respond the way that we hope. But a teacher or counselor could be that one adult who makes a true difference by not letting a child accept a self-defeating label, and by helping the child to identify and build on personal strengths.

References

Axline, Virginia M. (1964). *Dibs: In search of self.* New York: Ballantine.

Baldwin, Cynthia. (1997). Family systems and the single client. *The Family Journal, 5*(3), 254-256.

Elkind, David. (1981). *The hurried child: Growing up too fast too soon.* Reading, MA: Addison-Wesley.

Emery, Robert E. (1999). *Marriage, divorce, and children's adjustment* (2nd ed.). Thousand Oaks, CA: Sage.

Gil, Eliana. (1991). *The healing power of play: Working with abused children.* New York: Guilford Press.

Karr-Morse, Robin, & Wiley, Meridith S. (1997). *Ghosts from the nursery: Tracing the roots of violence.* New York: The Atlantic Monthly Press.

Miller, Alice. (1981). *Prisoners of childhood.* New York: Basic Books.

Moustakas, Clark E. (1975). *Who will listen?* New York: Ballantine Books.

Moustakas, Clark E. (1966). *The authentic teacher: Sensitivity and awareness in the classroom.* Cambridge, MA: H.A. Doyle.

Norton, Carol, & Norton, Byron. (1997). *Reaching children through play therapy.* Denver, CO: The Publishing Cooperative.

Straus, Martha B. (1999). *No-talk therapy for children and adolescents.* New York: Norton.

Sweeney, Daniel S. (1997). *Counseling children through the world of play.* Wheaton, IL: Tyndale House.

Tyndall-Lind, Ashley. (1999). Revictimization of children from violent families: Child centered theoretical formulation and play therapy treatment implications. *International Journal of Play Therapy, 8*(1), 9-25.

Van Fleet, Rise. (1994). *Filial therapy: Strengthening parent-child relationships through play.* Sarasota, FL: Professional Resource Press.

Parental Access Counseling Resources

There are no uniform ways to gain access to information about a particular state's counseling agencies. A county's mental health agency can provide information on specific programs and agencies for children in need of professional assistance. The agency might refer the family to behavior modification classes, or provide a list of counselors who specialize in long-term, nondirective play therapy. Contact your state's chapter of the Counseling Association, Association of Play Therapists, or Association of Social Workers for an area directory of counseling services (each association has a national branch if it is not possible to locate the state association).

To ascertain a counselor's qualifications ask questions related to credentials and training, and to the percentage of clients who are children. A play therapy counselor should welcome the involvement of parents, and ask for their insights.

Organizations and Web sites

American Counseling Association: www.counseling.org

Children's Defense Fund, 1520 New Hampshire Ave., N.W., Washington, DC, 20036

Early Childhood Educators and Family Web Corner: www.nauticom.net/www/cokids/index.html

Eliana Gil chat line for play therapists at Starbright Training Institute: www.nvgc.vt.edu/scripts/dialogue.dll?playther-c2

International Association for Play Therapy: www.a4pt.org

Institute for Trauma and Loss in Children: www.tlcinst.org

K.I.R.K. (Kreative and Innovative Resources for Kids), c/o Crystal Kuykendall, Ph.D., P.O. Box 60115, Potomac, MD 20859; E-Mail: Ckuykendall@aol.com

National Association of Social Workers: www.naswdc.org

National Center for Children in Poverty, Columbia University, 154 Haven Ave., New York, NY 10032-1180; phone: 212-304-7100; FAX 212-544-4200; E-Mail: nccp@columbia.edu; university Web site: http://cpmcnet.columbia.edu/dept/nccp

Therapeutic Tools, Games, and Ideas

Childswork/Childsplay, Center for Applied Psychology, 441 N. 5th St., Edison, NJ 08818, 135 Dupont St., P.O. Box 760, Plainview, NY 11803-0760, 1-800-962-1141, www.childwork.com

Creative Therapy Store, Western Psychological Services, 12031 Wilshire Blvd., Los Angeles, CA 90025-1251

Feelings Factory, 5089 St. Mary's St., Raleigh, NC 27605

Kidsrights, P.O. Box 851, Mt. Dora, FL 27605

Childcraft Education Corp., P.O. Box 3239, Lancaster, PA 17604; 800-631-5652

Toys To Grow On, P.O. Box 17, Long Beach, CA 90801

Toytrade@yahoo.com (affordable mental health tools, free catalog)

Uniquity, P.O. Box 6, Galt, CA 95623

Relevant Books for Children

Nemeroff, Marc A., & Annunziata, Jane. (1996). *A child's first book about play therapy.* Washington, DC: American Psychological Association.

This children's book, with its gentle illustrations, walks readers through the process of therapy and assuages concerns along the way.

Silverstein, Shel. (1979). *The missing piece.* New York: HarperCollins.

Silverstein, Shel. (1981). *The missing piece meets the big o.* New York: HarperCollins.

Both books take the reader on an imaginary journey of self-discovery and self-esteem.

Seuss, Dr. (1990). *Oh, the places you'll go!* New York: Random House.

A surprisingly useful book to help children identify fears and disappointments, and gain perspective on the journey of life.

Books for Parents

Barkley, Russell A., & Benton, Christine M. (1998). *Your defiant child.* New York: Guilford.

The book offers a formula for restoring communication between parent and child, including a wide variety of charts and exercises to aid the process.

Elkind, David. (1983). *Stress and its effects on learning.* Gaithersburg, MD: Aspen Systems.

Elkind, David. (1994). *Ties that stress: The new family imbalance.* Cambridge MA: Harvard University Press.

This interesting and knowledgeable author has published many works on the subject of children's development, education, and adults' responsibility for them.

Furth, Gregg M. (1988). *The secret world of drawings: Healing through art.* Boston: Sigo Press

A look inside the process of communication through art expression. This interesting text explains how trauma and fear may be expressed through symbols and themes.

Kuykendall, Crystal. (1992). *From rage to hope: Strategies for reclaiming black and Hispanic students.* Bloomington, IN: National Educational Service.

A counselor, teacher, author, and child advocate, Kuykendall offers an insightful, practical look at the rage of today's child and inspires the reader to reach out a helping hand.

Landreth, Garry L. (1991). *Play therapy: The art of the relationship.* Muncie, IN: Accelerated Development Inc.

Garry Landreth leads the field in play therapy and its applications. This is one of the many pieces he has written on the subject of children in therapy.

Minuchin, Patricia, Colapinto, Jorge, & Minuchin, Salvador. (1998). *Working with families of the poor.* New York: Guilford.

Drawing on years of experience working with the poor, the authors present case studies on the challenges and strengths of the family and community. Their invaluable recommendations come from the context of experiences working with families in a vast array of settings.

Moustakas, Clark E. (1956). *The teacher and the child: Personal interaction in the classroom.* New York: McGraw-Hill.

Moustakas, Clark E. (1979). *Psychotherapy with children: The living relationship.* New York: Harper.

Clark Moustakas has led generations of teachers and therapists to a better understanding of children—their development, how they communicate, and what we can do to form better relationships with them.

Pipher, Mary. (1994). *Reviving Ophelia.* New York: Ballantine.

The reader is carried through one terrifying case study after another in the world of adolescent girls. The accounts from counseling sessions are haunting. Missing, however, is any mention of body piercing, the effects of violent videos, or the dangers of the Internet, probably due to its publication date of nearly 10 years ago.

Epilogue

Kaoru Yamamoto

Even in this age of instant communication and rapid transportation, the world remains a large, awesome place, full of beauty and wonder. However, it can be rather bewildering and intimidating as well, especially for children.

Life, of course, is nothing without tension, and potential stressors are everywhere, in all varieties and intensities. As the combinations of personal and contextual factors are infinite, the specific coping and mastery approaches of the children, as well as adults' supportive, guiding, or restorative actions, must necessarily be based upon, and continuously adjusted to, unique individuals and their particular circumstances. Hopefully, the general discussion in this volume has provided a proper perspective and some basic principles about caring for children. The rest is entrusted with the initiative and ingenuity of the readers and of the children under their guidance.

What we need to keep in mind is the fundamental requirements for the healthy development of every person, succinctly summarized by Fromm (1971) three decades ago:

> Love for life will develop most in a society where there is: *security* in the sense that the basic material conditions for a dignified life are not threatened, *justice* in the sense that nobody can be an end for the purposes of another, and *freedom* in the sense that each man has the possibility to be an active and responsible member of society. (p. 57)

Alas, as current events continuously remind us, hardly anyone can boast of living up to that stated ideal.[1] As discouraging as the overall picture might appear to be, however, we have, at least in the realms of our professional assignments, a powerful ally in the almost limitless sense of trust and hope that young children bring to the world (Arendt, 1977). Also to be remembered is the fact that "the little organism is much tougher than we sometimes think" (Liebman, 1946, p. 123)—*provided*, of course, that the hope and trust of the young ones are reciprocated by the big people in what Winnicott (1986) characterized as "the good enough environment, which at the start of each individual's growth and development is a *sine qua non*" (p. 151). Therefore, "one of the most important of [the favorable] conditions is that the significant persons in a child's life have faith in [his or her] potentialities. The presence of this faith makes the difference between education and manipulation" (Fromm, 1967, p. 209).

We know that growing up is a scary, uncertain experience at any age accompanied by feelings of adventure and excitement, but also fear and trepidation. Nevertheless, sensing the trustworthiness of the grownups and their steady faith in them, children dare to advance. "One is afraid. Naturally. Who is not afraid of pure space—that breathtaking empty space of an open door? But despite fear, one goes through to the room beyond" (Lindbergh, 1955, p. 87).

The clarion call should be heard by all of us. It could not have been translated any more clearly than in this terse expression by Steiner (1997, p. 179):

> Receive the children in reverence,
> Educate them in love, and
> Send them forth in freedom.

ENDNOTE

1. Unfortunately, it has been abundantly clear that even the wealthier, more highly industrialized nation-states are far from fulfilling such desiderata. For instance, the United States has been jolted by very destructive, senseless acts like the 1995 bombing in Oklahoma City and the 1999 Columbine High School shooting incident in Denver. Also, this land of promise for some is a country marked with *Savage Inequalities* (Kozol, 1992) for others. It also harbors communities wherein young children were heard to preface their future plans with an expression, "*If* I grow up," rather than, "*When* I grow up" (Kotlowitz, 1991, p. x).

   Another case in point may be found in the United Kingdom. A recent, extensive study by the Joseph Rowntree Foundation reported that 24 percent of British households are under the poverty level in 1999, an increase of 10 percent from 1983. A total of 14.5 million people, out of a population of close to 60 million, cannot afford the three basic elements of normal existence, namely, three daily meals, sufficient clothing, and decently heated shelter. Four million children lack at least one of these three elements, while 2 million go without two of the necessities. One out of 50 must do without any new shoes, rain gear, or fruits and vegetables on a daily basis. One out of 25 pupils cannot purchase educational games, participate in extracurricular sports activities, or eat some fish or meat. The distance between the "haves" and "have-nots" continues to increase (Duplouich, 2000).

   In France, meanwhile, a report from the Economic and Social Council severely condemns the country's lack of progress in improving the life circumstances of the 3 million French (out of a population of 59 million) who have disabilities. The prevailing mentality is to "fit" the disabled to the existing environment, rather than to adapt the environment to fit those who have disabilities. For example, out of the 77 cities sampled in the spring of 2000, 48 had a public transport system totally unsuitable for the mobility-limited. A mere 7.3 percent of the bus lines proved accommodating. Children with disabilities appear to be identified as *handicapped* first, not as *children*. As a matter of fact, due to integration obstacles, two out of three such children are forced to stay out of school (Dore, 2000).

   Unfortunately, such somber examples can be readily repeated elsewhere to warn us against any complacency.

REFERENCES

Arendt, Hannah. (1977). *Between past and future.* New York: Penguin Books.

Dore, Christoph. (2000, September 12). Intégration des handicapés: L'échec français. *Le Figaro* (Paris), p. 11.

Duplouich, Jacques. (2000, September 12). La pauvreté progresse outre-Manche. *Le Figaro* (Paris), p. 4.

Fromm, Erich. (1967). *Man for himself.* New York: Fawcett.

Fromm, Erich. (1971). *The heart of man.* New York: Harper and Row.

Kotlowitz, Alex. (1991). *There are no children here.* New York: Doubleday.

Kozol, Jonathan. (1992). *Savage inequalities.* New York: Crown Publishers.

Liebman, Joshua. (1946). *Peace of mind.* New York: Simon and Schuster.

Lindbergh, Anne Morrow. (1955). *Gift from the sea.* New York: Vintage Books.

Steiner, Rudolf. (1997). *Gesamtausgabe,* vol. 269, p. 179. [*Quellenangabe*, p. 241.] Dornach, Switzerland: Rudolf Steiner Nachlassverwaltung.

Winnicott, D. W. (1986). *Home is where we start from.* New York: W. W. Norton.

Contributing Authors

David P. Colachico, Ed.D. Associate Professor and Director of Special Education, Azusa Pacific University, Azusa, California.

Beth Houskamp, Ph.D. Associate Professor, Department of Graduate Psychology, Azusa Pacific University, Azusa, California.

Ross Huff, M.A. School Psychologist, Duarte School District, Duarte, California.

Marc C. Mahlios, Ph.D. Professor, Department of Teaching & Leadership, University of Kansas, Lawrence, Kansas.

Marilyn M. Maxson, Ph.D. Deceased. (Indiana State University, Terre Haute, Indiana.)

Gail McEachron, Ph.D. Associate Professor, School of Education, College of William and Mary, Williamsburg, Virginia.

Maria A. Pacino, Ed.D. Professor and Chair, Department of Advanced Studies, Azusa Pacific University, Azusa, California.

Beverly Hardcastle Stanford, Ph.D. Professor, Graduate Education, Director of the Center for Research on Ethics and Values, Azusa Pacific University, Azusa, California.

Alice V. Watkins, Ph.D. Dean, School of Education and Behavioral Studies, Azusa Pacific University, Azusa, California.

Kaoru Yamamoto, Ph.D. Professor Emeritus, University of Colorado - Denver, Colorado.

Sherry Lawry Young, M.A., LPC. Program Director, Bridge Builders Counseling, Port Huron, Michigan.